P9-CDJ-591

# WINNING
## AT
# RETAIL

# WINNING
## AT
# RETAIL

Developing a
Sustained Model
for
Retail Success

**WILLARD N. ANDER
AND NEIL Z. STERN**

**WILEY**

JOHN WILEY & SONS, INC.

Copyright © 2004 by Willard N. Ander and Neil Z. Stern. All rights reserved.

Published by John Wiley & Sons, Inc., Hoboken, New Jersey.
Published simultaneously in Canada.

No part of this publication may be reproduced, stored in a retrieval system, or transmitted in any form or by any means, electronic, mechanical, photocopying, recording, scanning, or otherwise, except as permitted under Section 107 or 108 of the 1976 United States Copyright Act, without either the prior written permission of the Publisher, or authorization through payment of the appropriate per-copy fee to the Copyright Clearance Center, Inc., 222 Rosewood Drive, Danvers, MA 01923, (978) 750-8400, fax (978) 646-8600, or on the web at www.copyright.com. Requests to the Publisher for permission should be addressed to the Permissions Department, John Wiley & Sons, Inc., 111 River Street, Hoboken, NJ 07030, (201) 748-6011, fax (201) 748-6008.

Limit of Liability/Disclaimer of Warranty: While the publisher and author have used their best efforts in preparing this book, they make no representations or warranties with respect to the accuracy or completeness of the contents of this book and specifically disclaim any implied warranties of merchantability or fitness for a particular purpose. No warranty may be created or extended by sales representatives or written sales materials. The advice and strategies contained herein may not be suitable for your situation. The publisher is not engaged in rendering professional services, and you should consult a professional where appropriate. Neither the publisher nor author shall be liable for any loss of profit or any other commercial damages, including but not limited to special, incidental, consequential, or other damages.

For general information on our other products and services please contact our Customer Care Department within the United States at (800) 762-2974, outside the United States at (317) 572-3993 or fax (317) 572-4002.

Wiley also publishes its books in a variety of electronic formats. Some content that appears in print may not be available in electronic books. For more information about Wiley products, visit our web site at *www.Wiley.com*.

*Library of Congress Cataloging-in-Publication Data:*
Ander, Jr., Willard N.
   Winning at retail : developing a sustained model for retail success / Willard N. Ander, Jr. and Neil Z. Stern.
      p. cm.
ISBN 0-471-47357-X (cloth)
1. Retail trade—Management.   I. Stern, Neil.   II. Title.
HF5429.A655 2004
658.8'7—dc22                                              2004002264

Printed in the United States of America
10 9 8 7 6 5 4 3 2

# CONTENTS

# PREFACE

*"How did you go bankrupt?"*
*"Gradually, then suddenly."*

ERNEST HEMINGWAY,
*THE SUN ALSO RISES*

Montgomery Ward. Woolworth. Florsheim. County Seat. Service Merchandise. Bradlees. Builders Square. eToys. The retail landscape is littered with the bodies of companies who simply were not good enough to compete for a customer's business anymore. Many of these companies were once the shining stars of business, the subjects of glowing praise from analysts and often-positive case studies in books just like this one. What happened to them? They fell into the Black Hole of Retailing, the place where losing retailers go to die.

The sad fact of these companies' demise is that their death may have been avoidable. They failed to react to the signs around them and positively change their business while they still had time. Most companies eventually react to their fate, but way too late. Consistently winning companies react before Wall Street tells them to, before their sales volume is in permanent tailspin, before a competitor grows too big and too powerful, and, most important, before customers have given up and moved on to spend their retail dollars at a multitude of other choices.

The "B-Est" retailers—those with a defined position in the marketplace—have determined how to carve out and own a place in

# Preface

the customer's mind. They fiercely defend this space but are also astute enough to recognize when it's time to find something new.

All retailers are destined to decline: There is a force at work—an inevitable retail life cycle—that leads to certain failure unless something dramatic occurs to interrupt the flow and change the outcome. There is a natural inflection point in the life of every concept and every retailer. Failure to react at this critical point can lead to a painful downward spiral. React properly, and companies can experience a rebirth and live to fight another day. The best retailers are those that recognize the necessary role of business reinvention and seek to stay ahead of the pack.

Unfortunately, most retailers fail to react to the inflection point, fail to listen to what their customers are trying to tell them, and are generally content to get by with being pretty good. Being pretty good is an invitation to enter the loser's playground, an area in which many retailers dwell today. It's not a far ride from the loser's playground to the Black Hole.

This book is not based on fancy academic theories that have no place in the real world. *Winning at Retail* is a rather boring title, we have to admit. It's not going to win any awards for creativity. There are no cute parables—not a single fish or piece of cheese. This book is based on McMillan|Doolittle's long history of documenting retail's winners and losers. It's also based on our experience consulting with the world's best-known retail and service companies. We have had some wonderful successes with our clients, and we learned from those experiences; we have also had some failures along the way, and learned from those as well. In this book we talk about stores and about customers. We discuss what separates the winners and losers, and we extract key lessons from each.

For retailers, this book is a must-read to understand where your company stands in its life cycle and to begin to plan new courses of action. For suppliers, you'll find that the lessons in the retail world are very similar to your own. You will also want to know whom to align with, now and into the future. For retail investors, real estate companies, financial institutions, and others closely aligned with the retail world, Est offers an early warning system—well before earnings begin to decelerate and decline. Finally, we are all customers—all experts in an intimate way in this fascinating $3 trillion a year business.

We pull no punches—that's not our style. We're candid, straightforward, and passionate about the business that we've devoted our careers to understanding. We are true to McMillan|Doolittle's intrepid motto: "Occasionally wrong, but never in doubt!"

Why are we writing this book now? As we will demonstrate, the retail business is getting tougher than ever. Consumers have access to an unprecedented number of choices and are becoming more selective about where they shop. Retail space per capita has reached unprecedented levels, and the consumer, once buoyed by exuberant spending in the late 1990s, is coming back down to earth. This equation of too many retailers chasing too few consumer dollars has made for some painful times for the nation's retail companies. Only the best are thriving now, and we expect that to be the case in the future. Few retailers will be able to survive in the coming years without excelling in meeting consumer needs.

Why should you listen to what we have to say? We have a long history of participating, analyzing, and consulting—we are grounded in both the reality of being a retailer and the forces that swirl around the industry.

## MCMILLAN | DOOLITTLE: A BRIEF HISTORY

Norm McMillan and Sid Doolittle, the founders of McMillan| Doolittle, first worked together in the late 1970s, when Norm took the assignment of leading one of many turnaround efforts at Montgomery Ward & Co. Sid, a veteran of Chicago-based Wards, was part

# Preface

of that team. In the span of four decades, Wards had gone from being one of the nation's largest merchants to being a retailer in desperate need of a turnaround. Part of Norm and Sid's mission was to survey the retail landscape, figure out what separated the winners from the losers, and then help Montgomery Ward re-create itself as a winner. A very big task, indeed.

The two men brought different skills to the job. Norm began his career in advertising, and then cut his retailing teeth developing a strategy for a struggling discount chain called Target. Before joining Wards, Norm led a team in the mid-1970s that articulated a new mission and vision for Target. (The result was a strategy the retailer hasn't strayed from yet, as it's grown from being a struggling unit of a department store company to becoming the nation's fifth-largest retailer, with nearly $40 billion in sales.) Norm created a then (and still) revolutionary document, titled *Guides for Growth,* which helped steer Target's course as a fashion-driven discounter.

Sid had spent his entire career with Wards. He ran merchandising, buying, and catalog operations and also participated in long-term strategic planning. The two men shared a passion for retail stores and retail customers. Norm was proficient in the then-unnamed concepts of positioning and branding, and he understood what those things mean for retailers. Sid knew the day-in, day-out of retail and understood how to make stores and catalogs run smoothly and profitably.

Wards rallied a little, as it would do numerous times before finally closing down in early 2001. Sid left Wards in 1981 to become a retail entrepreneur, cofounding a regional chain in the nascent warehouse club industry. Norm went on to help position retailers owned by a company called Household Merchandising, including such well-known chains as Vons supermarkets and Coast-to-Coast hardware stores.

The two men reunited for a brief time at Household before they set out on their own in 1986, forming McMillan|Doolittle LLP, a retail consulting firm.

## MCMILLAN|DOOLITTLE'S POINT OF VIEW

From the beginning, McMillan|Doolittle has had a few core principles:

- We preach positioning, which we define as owning something in customers' minds. It also entails identifying specific customers and delivering something meaningful to them that the competition isn't.
- We track winners and losers. Soon after Norm and Sid founded the firm, they introduced a newsletter called *Retail Watch,* with articles about the stores they toured. We still publish *Retail Watch* every month, in which we analyze and critique retail stores around the world, discussing new concepts and formats in categories as diverse as hardware stores and restaurants.
- Another core principle of our practice is the notion that retail is all about *customers.* From the beginning, we've worked with supermarkets, gas stations, and department stores, because we've always contended that customer behavior and trends remain constant, regardless of the retail format. Our customer focus also has allowed us to do work for companies that serve retailers, such as consumer product manufacturers, advertising agencies, investment banks, and real estate companies. No matter the client, our commonsense approach to retail remains the same: Give customers more of what they want and less of what they don't want.
- Finally, we strive to be honest and straightforward. We also keep things simple, and we tell it like it is. There's no place in retail for fancy and elaborate theories. Likewise, there's no place in retail for somebody who's hell-bent on using a million-dollar word when a ten-cent one will do just fine.

# Preface

Retailers have neither the time nor the inclination to digest euphemisms and sugar-coated remedies.

Our candor is a value to clients. It has made us sought-after speakers and commentators on the retail industry and has made *Retail Watch* a popular publication. Retailers use *Retail Watch* to track competitors, to learn about new store concepts, and to get ideas about best practices and worst practices. Real estate brokers and consumer product manufacturers use it as a tip sheet to scout for potential clients. What makes *Retail Watch* work, in our opinion, is our opinions.

We have a point of view, and we tell it. We don't mince words. We don't hesitate to voice our likes and dislikes, our concerns, and our doubts. Of course, we've upset some clients and potential clients, but we believe that our unabashed, uncensored opinions are what makes the newsletter valuable. (In fact, we've been called the Siskel and Ebert of retailing—although we never adopted a thumbs-up, thumbs-down system.)

With more than 17 years' worth of articles, *Retail Watch* represents an unparalleled body of work about retail stores—particularly new concepts and prototypes for established retailers. When we write about stores, we focus on the retailer's strategy and positioning. We also look for basic execution, but most important, we watch customers to get a sense of store performance. An accountant would insist that we review the books before assessing sales and profits. Of course, there's a reason why accountants make crummy retailers. The number of customers in a store, where they are, and whether they're leaving with purchases or empty-handed tells the trained eye a great deal about a retailer's performance. We'd venture to say that you wouldn't find many better-trained eyes than ours. We're like the art critic who explains how to tell whether a painting is good: "When you've seen 50,000 paintings, you know whether the 50,001st is any good."

Music fans love to tell about having seen a famous band long before it hit the big time: "I knew them when . . ." We're like that with stores. Name a successful retailer in the second half of the twentieth century, and chances are that a partner with McMillan|Doolittle visited one of their first stores, studied its strategies, and gauged customer reactions. We probably also wrote an article about it—complete with discreetly taken photographs—for *Retail Watch*. For instance, Norm McMillan visited the first Home Depot in Atlanta. Sid Doolittle toured Price Club in San Diego, the nation's first warehouse club store. We worked with Staples when the retailer had only two stores in the suburbs of Boston. We visited the first Wal-Mart supercenter in Washington, Missouri, as well as Wal-Mart's first attempt at a supermarket/discount store combination, HyperMart USA, in Garland, Texas. We make it a point to visit stores that break new ground. That's a thrill to us, because it's like glimpsing the future.

One of the greatest things about the retail business is its immediacy. Inventory is bought and put on a certain shelf in a certain aisle at a certain price at a certain time of year. Soon after the store opens, the retailer has a pretty good sense of whether he or she has done all those things right or wrong. Retail executives don't have to wait years to learn whether they've won or lost. In retailing, fortunes are literally made and lost every day based on thousands of seemingly insignificant contact points with customers. Were they able to park close enough to the store? Was the parking lot well lit? Could they easily find what they were looking for? Was the price competitive with another store two blocks away? Were they able to get through checkout quickly?

That's what retail is all about. It's not about poring over balance sheets and scrutinizing sales figures. These types of details make retail a tough and demanding business. In reality, it's simple. Retail is about looking at stores and looking at customers. If retailers do a good job of that, they are not going to be wrong very often.

While that sounds pretty easy, it's actually extremely difficult.

# Preface

Due to the nature of the business, a retailer has to make thousands of little decisions every day—and very few big decisions. That makes it difficult for retailers to think ahead five years, even one year, because the day-to-day business is so consuming. It has been said that retail involves looking three months into the past (what sold and what didn't) and one hour into the future. That's why so many retailers miss the big picture and fail miserably at long-term strategy and vision.

What we most enjoy about our place in retail is that we live in the thrill of the business's immediacy while also exploring the strategies and positioning crucial for future success. We have the luxury of being able to look forward, while many of our retail clients do not. It provides us with a unique perspective to try to bridge that gap, because we understand day-to-day retail issues, yet we also understand that stores must develop forward-looking strategies or risk not being around in the future.

# ACKNOWLEDGMENTS

We would like to extend our heartfelt thanks and gratitude to Norm McMillan and Sid Doolittle, our teachers, mentors, and guides, who continue to provide the heart and soul of McMillan|Doolittle's retail practice. We would also like to thank Eddie Baeb, former retail reporter for *Crain's Chicago Business* and current staff writer for Bloomberg News, for his invaluable assistance in shaping the content and tone of the book and for conducting much of the background research that shaped the foundation. We would like to thank the extended family of current and past McMillan|Doolittle partners, affiliates, and clients for providing many of the thoughts, examples, and ideas that form the foundation of this book. And special thanks to Felicia Glinstra and Alison Perkins for helping to develop the data and charts and for generally putting up with us during the process of writing this book.

# PART I
# The Theory

# CHAPTER ONE

# EST: A COMPASS TO AVOID RETAIL'S BLACK HOLE

**B**eware the Black Hole!

The Black Hole is the place where retail companies that are no longer relevant to customers go to die. As you may recall from high school physics, a black hole is a region in space where the gravitational pull is so strong that not even light can escape. That is also an apt description for retailers that have not established themselves as the best store for customers looking to fulfill a specific need: Once they are in the Retail Black Hole, it's next to impossible to get out.

In recent years, the number of retailers entering the Black Hole increased as store productivity slowed and competition increased. Not only the small, regional chains were failing. Big-name retailers with hundreds of stores—some nationwide—were going out of business.

Chapter 11 bankruptcy has become practically a household phrase among U.S. consumers, with Kmart filing the largest such case in business history. Unfortunately, so-called Chapter 22 is becoming nearly as common—retailers who restructured their businesses once, only to meet the same bankruptcy fate a few years later down the line.

Frankly, it made our Black Hole presentations better, and we spend more than our fair share of time working with the press to explain what these failures mean to retailing and to consumers. It also became clear to us that these stores were failing because they were not properly responding to the way customers were changing: They had not become best at anything (or had ceased to fill that role) for customers.

Now, because of the Internet, extraordinary access to capital, and nearly instantaneous worldwide communications, retail change is happening faster than ever. Winning chains such as Wal-Mart are continuing to grab market share at an unprecedented rate, while foreign retailers with strong track records, such as Ikea, Zara, and H&M, are becoming a larger part of America's retail landscape. Entire retail categories—such as variety stores, regional discount stores, regional electronics chains, and catalog showrooms—have all but disappeared. Once-successful retailers are becoming obsolete at a fast pace.

No retailer is immune. Kmart, the nation's third-largest discount store chain, was forced to file Chapter 11 bankruptcy in January 2002. Less than a decade ago, Kmart was the nation's second-largest retailer. Other large retail chains that may seem a long way from the brink are also in peril. That's because stores like Kmart are adrift in a place that we call the Sea of Mediocrity. These stores aren't best at anything, and they don't have a distinct or sharply defined customer proposition.

It's not easy staying on top, either. Over the years, the examples we use to illustrate winning retailers have gone through constant change. Role model retailers like Circuit City and Toys "R" Us have fallen on hard times, failing to react to their own individual inflection points. Even a gold standard retailer like Home Depot is looking into the rearview mirror, as nimbler competitors like Lowe's do a better job of responding to consumer needs. The immediacy of the retail business and the customer's response to a retailer's offer create a constant scorecard with which to measure success. Comparable store sales figures (sales of identical stores currently versus a year ago) provide a running commentary on the industry. We know, almost in real time (Amazon.com showcases a gift meter on its web site), how a company is performing.

The ebb and flow of successful companies is hardly unique to the world of retail. The same phenomena take place every day in any business that serves the consumer. How, though, can one explain this logically, so companies can stay ahead of the curve instead of simply reacting to it? In too many cases, by the time a company is nearing Chapter 11 (or the Black Hole), it is way too late to effect meaningful change with the consumer or on Wall Street. The key, of course, is to determine trouble before it occurs and act accordingly.

## EST DEFINED

The breakthrough for McMillan|Doolittle was our drive to articulate retail success in a straightforward way and make sense of the seemingly random changes we were witnessing on a daily basis in the retail world. Our goal was to simplify rather than complicate. We worked hard to be plainspoken and to come up with a better way of explaining things. Ultimately, that led to the development in the early 1990s of what we call the *Est theory for retail success.*

The Est theory derives from the word *best,* and it essentially says that a retailer must be best at one proposition that's important to a specific group of customers. Retailers must strive for a specific positioning to a specific set of customers rather than attempting to be great at everything to everybody. To accomplish this might mean targeting a specific customer at the exclusion of others, giving up on merchandise categories that today might still be yielding profitable sales, or forgoing short-term growth and profits with an eye toward long-term success. These ideas were heretical for most retailers at the time and are concepts that most struggle with even today.

Est originated through an analytical exercise in which we systematically studied winning retailers (as defined by sales growth and profitability) to determine what made them tick. As we tried to discern the key attributes that made them successful, a rather startling pattern emerged. In those companies that had a singular defining characteristic from a consumer perspective, we saw well-above-average financial results, even among companies pursuing seemingly disparate aims. Companies for which we could not isolate any one defining reason for being almost inevitably wound up somewhere in the middle of the pack. It became clear to us that being the best with consumers had a clear impact on the bottom line.

Do you really have to be *best* to succeed? We are often asked that by our retail and service company clients who proudly show how *good* they are in many areas. As Jim Collins proclaimed in his book *Good to Great,* "Good is the enemy of great." We agree, and we take it one step further. "Pretty good" are words retailers should dread, because if you are *not* an Est retailer and you're still in business, that's probably how customers describe you: "Pretty good." That means customers have other stores they'd rather shop. Sooner or later (most likely sooner) they will find those stores or those stores will find them, and they won't come back to you. Today's time-starved shoppers don't frequent mediocre stores.

Clearly, customers have less time to shop. They are also more knowledgeable about the products they want to buy and the stores that sell them. They have more choices of where to shop than ever before.

The customers who still frequent mediocre stores probably do so because of a historic attachment—it's where they or their parents always shopped. Or they were attracted to the mediocre store because of a sales promotion. Or they simply didn't have the time or energy to drive to a preferred store. Finally, being handy to where they live or work certainly helps. We can hardly dispute the old retail adage—location, location, location. Yet consumer research indicates that it is the proverbial kiss of death if location is the primary reason customers shop at your stores—someone else can always get closer.

Whatever the case, these types of customer relationships do not have a bright future, which is why pretty good isn't good enough anymore.

Many of the stores now enshrined in our Black Hole memorial were pretty good stores. (See Figure 1.1.) Montgomery Ward, for instance, ranked third or fourth by consumers as places they'd likely shop for various items. While Wards wasn't anything-Est, at least it was a close also-ran in some categories. That doesn't sound too bad. Not many people *hated* Wards—but even worse, they were simply indifferent. How's Wards on price? "Pretty good." How's Wards on service? "Pretty good." How's Wards on fashion? "Pretty good."

**FIGURE 1.1**   Black Hole Memorial

How's Wards on assortment? "Pretty good." Those kinds of results from customer surveys may have seemed pretty reassuring to Wards' executives. Actually, being pretty good at lots of things was the foundation of the modern era of mass retailing for general-merchandise stores. It was a pretty good formula into the 1980s. It's not anymore.

Pretty good stores cannot satisfy increasingly demanding customers. Pretty good stores also cannot compete with today's sharpest retail chains. Stores like Wal-Mart, Target, Costco, and Kohl's have raised customer expectations. Falling short of expectations means not satisfying customers, and that's the most direct path to the Black Hole.

## EST IS NOT A MARKETING TOOL

Est is not simply a "marketing thing," a way to position a company in advertising and external communications. The buzzword today is *branding,* and while we believe in the concept, too many companies confuse the articulation of a marketing and/or design message with the essence of the company. Est Retailers devote themselves with laserlike focus to their core customer proposition, what we call their *Est position.* They commit employees from the top to the bottom of their organization to that position. They communicate that positioning to their customers and execute it relentlessly at the store level. Est retailers also base strategic and day-to-day operational decisions on their positioning. An Est positioning is not simply the marketing message du jour—it is a way of life for successful retailers.

Wal-Mart is the quintessential example. Everything Wal-Mart does is focused on enhancing its position as the low-price leader. With its "Always Low Prices" tagline and "Everyday Low Price" positioning, Wal-Mart wins with customers on price. Yet this is not merely an advertising proposition—the drive for lower prices for the consumer defines every action that the company takes. It is at the heart of Wal-Mart's mission, its very reason for being. Sam Walton founded what is now the world's largest company (period, not just in retail) on the simple belief that customers would like to pay less for the products they purchase and that ordinary folks should have the opportunity to buy products that make their lives better. Every single action the company takes is measured against these fundamental principles.

We call that particular Est *Cheap-Est* (and it has served companies like Wal-Mart very well). The other Est positions that win customers are *Big-Est*, having the largest assortment of product in a specific merchandise category; *Hot-Est*, having the right products just as customers begin to buy them in volume; *Easy-Est*, having the proper combination of products and services that makes shopping easy; and *Quick-Est*, organizing the store to make the shopping trip as quick and efficient as possible. (See Figure 1.2.)

**FIGURE 1.2**   Est Model

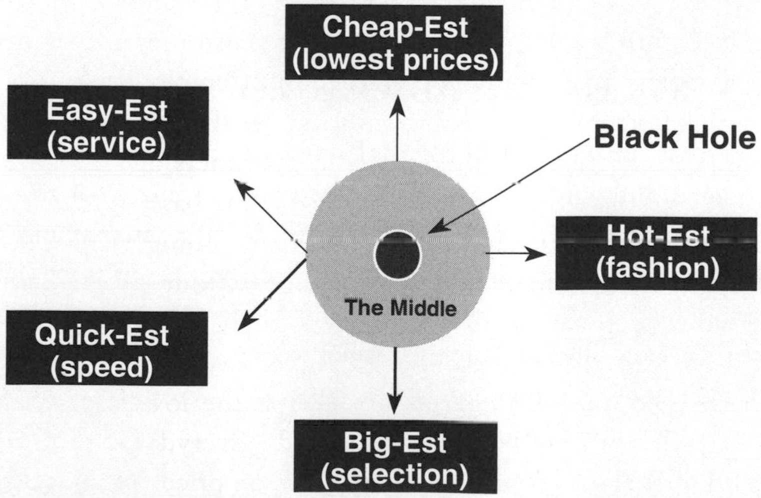

## THE INTRODUCTION OF EST

Norm McMillan, one of the company's founding partners, first presented the Est theory in the early 1990s at an international food industry trade show in France. It played well in Paris (and subsequently Peoria), and we've been using and fine-tuning the model ever since. The theory has resonated with our clients (and to audiences throughout the world) for more than a decade because its message is easy to grasp and is actionable.

By further studying these companies, we also recognized they had done much more than carve out a niche. They weren't simply the best among their rivals by default. These retailers had devoted their organizations from top to bottom to becoming the best in one particular area. It was the driving force of their businesses. Once we identified what the winning retailers strove to be best at for customers, the Est theory was born.

We liked the model we had hatched. It made sense to us. But we were waiting for someone to fire a silver bullet, to raise a question or example that Est couldn't easily answer or explain. We're still waiting.

## DOES EST CHANGE? ABSOLUTELY

We created Quick-Est in the mid-1990s to recognize the growing importance of saving customers time and to recognize that retailers can win by focusing on providing customers with time savings as a key benefit. While this may have always been true, consumer trends (working women, less free time) finally made time a critical currency that we could effectively model. Who's to say that another driving element won't emerge as the consumer continues to evolve? However, we are cautious in screening between a fad and a key consumer trend.

## EST: A Compass to Avoid Retail's Black Hole

In the mid-1990s, we also heard from people who thought we should add a new position to recognize the emergence of entertainment-focused retail stores. Remember "retail-tainment?" At the time, everyone from restaurants to retail stores packaged entertainment as a key selling factor. We considered adding categories like "Exciting-Est" or "Entertaining-Est," but ultimately we rejected the idea because, regardless of how exciting it is, a store's ultimate purpose is to sell merchandise. Customers need a more rational reason to visit a store than its entertainment value.

If all a store had going for it was that it was best at entertainment, could it win? We don't think so—and the customers have voted, too. Warner Brothers shuttered their once-exciting retail stores, and many "eater-tainment" restaurants have scaled back their growth.

We believe a store can win by being clearly best in one of five critical areas: *assortment* (Big-Est), *price* (Cheap-Est), *fashion* (Hot-Est), *solution-oriented service* (Easy-Est), or *speed-oriented service* (Quick-Est). There are other possible niche Est positions (such as Fine-Est, for the high-quality, luxury retail segments), but successful retailers today serving the masses can clearly be defined by one of these core Est positions.

Does an Est retailer exclude a focus on those other retail elements? Of course not. As we discuss in later chapters, all retailers must provide a base level of competency across all factors critical to the consumers. The real winners are the ones who found an Est that they could own.

The advent of e-commerce also forced us to reexamine Est. Remember e-tailers? Certainly, this was no flash-in-the-pan trend like "retail-tainment." We studied e-commerce and how customers shop online, and we found that e-commerce and some of its winners (Amazon.com, Priceline) in no way disproved the Est theory. In fact, we believe the theory applies as plainly online as it does in the bricks-and-mortar world.

As we said, the Est model will change over time, but the underlying theory is likely to stay intact. For instance, as customers and competitors evolve, it's possible that Big-Est will no longer be a position that's sufficient to win. Also, if customers become increasingly driven by safety, quality, or product integrity, we may add an Est position to reflect that. Quality, or getting the job done right the first time, is a critical element, particularly in the retail services industry. Part of the power of the theory is that it can easily be altered or adapted, yet still be true to its essence.

Fortune 500 companies such as McDonald's, Procter & Gamble, and The Limited have put Est to work in their businesses. That's because in addition to explaining what it takes to succeed in retail—a critical lesson in these perilous times for the retail industry—the Est model can be used in several actionable ways:

- Est is an analytical tool that companies, both retailers and nonretailers, can use to determine where they stand with customers and how they compare with competitors. In a very simple format, it provides a diagnostic tool to understand where a company stands.
- It is also a prescriptive tool for a company to identify market niches and growth opportunities. If there are available niches, it points them out. If there's not a clear opening available (which is increasingly becoming the case), it identifies where the business will have to come from.
- Finally, Est can be used to form a company's strategic foundation. It's a way to focus strategic decisions and day-to-day operations on one big idea—the Est position.

The Est model is a powerful tool that helps retailers avoid the Black Hole and also helps them attain growth, profits, and enduring success.

## PUTTING EST TO WORK

Our two favorite real-world examples of putting Est to work are Target and Vons supermarkets.

Soon after Target adopted its better-quality strategy in the mid-1970s, the company's chairman at the time stood before a meeting of several hundred company executives and held up a pair of sneakers. He described the shoes as shoddy. The soles fell off easily, and several customers had complained. Then he asked which buyer had bought these shoes. A timid hand went up. The buyer explained that he got a great deal. The shoes were closeout items from China. Target bought them for $2 and was selling them for $8. It was profitable for the company and a great price for customers. A relatively small number of customers had complained, especially considering the phenomenal price. The chairman listened, then asked, "What does our strategy say?" No answer. "It says Target sells quality merchandise." At that time, discount stores were known for selling shoddy products, but that's not what Target aspired to be. The chairman then instructed the buyer to have all the shoes immediately removed from the stores and destroyed. The chairman chose a very public place to make a point about positioning and the importance of being true to an Est position, even at the cost of passing up profit opportunities.

In the mid-1980s, we helped Vons supermarkets develop a new retail food concept called Pavilions. It was to be positioned as the "fresh, fashion-forward supermarket for the masses." We suggested that to win at that position required Pavilions to become friendlier to moms. One thing we learned from customer surveys: Moms who shopped at Pavilions hated the fact that gum-ball machines were near the storefront and that so much candy was for sale at the checkouts. Essentially, these customers felt that the candy instigated fights between mothers and their children. We told Pavilions to get rid of the gum-ball machines because they were causing problems for key customers. The store managers howled—gum-ball machines and checkout aisle candy provided a great source of income from square footage that would otherwise be inactive. Still, the executives mapping out strategy recognized the importance of simple positioning messages. They got rid of the gum-ball machines and even instituted a couple of candy-free checkout aisles. It told us that Vons executives were serious about positioning Pavilions, because they would not let short-term profits get in the way of doing something right for customers. (We still have one of those old machines in our office—a reminder that positioning is never an easy exercise.)

Having an Est position makes it easier for retailers to communicate effectively to customers and their associates and helps the stores execute consistently. In turn, consistently executing on an Est proposition further strengthens and enhances the Est position. Each example of truly executing Est confirms the store's core purpose. For Hot-Est retailers, it means continually demonstrating that you're the place for the latest fashions or newest products. Once or twice may be a fluke. Year in and year out, it becomes an Est.

It is a perpetuating cycle, but it can happen only after a retailer commits to being great for specific consumers and not so great for others. Nothing is more alarming to us than having clients boast that their stores are good at everything and are shopped by everyone. It means they really don't understand the most fundamental principle of effective positioning.

While the Est theory may appear relatively benign and somewhat self-evident, it's actually quite radical. It runs contrary to the notion of trying to do everything for customers, and it upends the age-old axiom that "the customer is always right." Customers aren't always right. Customers would want a store to have the lowest prices, the best service, the largest selection, and the latest fashions. While that may sound like a winning proposition and a goal worth pursuing, we've seen lots of retailers go out of business chasing that kind of strategy. It's simply not a profitable proposition to try to be everything customers want. In fact, though, many retailers do try. They want to be great—they just don't know what to be great at and for whom.

Of course, we don't mean to suggest that retailers should not listen to customers. We are saying that retailers must listen selectively—focusing on the real needs of their core customers. Keep these questions in mind as filters: Who are core customers and who are not? What do core customers want more of? What do they want less of? Deliver more of what core customers want and less of what they don't want. That way, you will be great at a limited number of things. You also will avoid the trap of trying to be all things to all people.

It is no coincidence that the intersection of all five Est positions is right in the middle of the Est model circle. We call it the Black Hole of Retailing. A retailer that tries to be great at everything, at all Ests, may actually wind up good in some areas. But that retailer isn't likely to be best at everything—and most likely won't be best at anything.

For reasons both practical and empirical, it is impossible to succeed in being Est in all key consumer attributes. Great retailers understand that practical sacrifices must be made to achieve an Est positioning. Even if the retailer somehow manages to be best in several areas, it won't make any money, because achieving and maintaining each Est position requires heavy resources and large financial commitments.

## THE PROOF IS IN THE RESULTS

Yes, concepts like Est and the Black Hole are catchy and memorable. However, in the pragmatic world of retail consulting, theories don't go very far. Companies demand proof that taking an Est direction is the right financial path. Est does have a powerful impact on the financial results of companies. This is not an academic theory—it is based on empirical proof that Est companies outperform and outgrow those that strive to be just pretty good.

Talking dollars and sense, the results for Est retailers over the 10 years from 1993 through 2002 dramatically prove our point. (See Table 1.1.) During this period of time, the broadly defined retail industry in the United States grew at a compounded rate of 5.3 percent, with sales rising from $1.7 trillion to nearly $2.7 trillion. A selected market basket of Est retailers grew at well over double that rate during the same time period, with standout performers maintaining growth rates of well over 15 percent. (See Table 1.2.) The best performers on our Est charts grew at well over 30 percent, or six times that of the market.

What about profits? Est retailers deliver on the bottom line as well. Looking at the top 100 retailers in the United States reveals that the average net profit as a percent of sales is 2.72 percent. Breaking out the Est performers shows that they are averaging profits in

**TABLE 1.1**  Retail Industry Sales Performance

|  | 1993 ($ billions) | 2002 ($ billions) | Compound Annual Growth Rate (%), 1993–2002 |
|---|---|---|---|
| General, apparel, furniture, and other retail sales | $574 | $935 | 5.6 |
| Retail and food services sales total (excl. motor vehicle and parts dealers) | $1,720 | $2,727 | 5.3 |
| Retail sales total (incl. motor vehicle and parts dealers) | $1,986 | $3,245 | 5.6 |
| Retail sales total (excl. motor vehicle and parts dealers) | $1,504 | $2,393 | 5.3 |

*Source:* U.S. Census Bureau.

# EST: A Compass to Avoid Retail's Black Hole

**TABLE 1.2**    Est Retailer Sales Performance

| Retailer* | 1993 Sales ($ billions) | 2002 Sales ($ billions) | Compound Annual Growth Rate (%), 1993–2002 |
|---|---|---|---|
| Cheap-Est: Wal-Mart | $55 | $245 | 16 |
| Big-Est: Home Depot | $9 | $58 | 23 |
| Hot-Est: Target | $19 | $43 | 13 |
| Easy-Est: Kohl's | $1 | $9 | 24 |
| Quick-Est: Walgreens | $8 | $29 | 15 |

*Discount stores only.

excess of 4 percent, on average. Those in the middle? Their profits creep along at just over 1 percent, teetering precariously close to the Black Hole. Can an average retailer produce above–average profits? Absolutely—for a while. Ultimately, however, the lack of a defined positioning leads to stagnant sales growth, which leads to declining profits.

As this book progresses, we talk both theory and results. Winning with customers also means winning on the balance sheet. Getting to Est is the most enduring way of achieving both.

# CHAPTER TWO

# CUSTOMERS ARE #1

## Now It's Time for Retailers to Start Treating Them That Way

We begin by taking a bit of our own advice and discussing the most important (yet often overlooked) element of retail success: the customer. We also begin by setting the precedent of pulling no punches and debunking some of the many myths that surround retailing.

Retailers are quick to pronounce, "We put customers first!" or "Our customers are number one!" or "We provide great customer service!" In fact, we have yet to review a retailer's annual report, mission statement, or formal communications that does not contain some wonderful statement about how the customer is the most important part of its business. While these statements make great fodder for annual reports and break-room bulletin boards, they are, unfortunately, mostly fiction.

## THE MYTHS OF CUSTOMER SERVICE

Few retailers understand what it means to put customers first. Even fewer actually do it. Customer retail service is broken—just ask any customer. That's because, for many retailers, customer service is really a myth.

Let's expose some of the great myths of retailing concerning customer service.

**Myth 1:**    Retailers put customers first.

**Reality:**    Retailers put their own interest way ahead of customers' interests.

It is evident in the way retailers merchandise their stores, how they organize departments, how they staff their stores, and how they often don't keep adequate inventory.

Do retailers present their goods so that a customer can shop easily? Hardly. Walk into any department store and ask the first sales associate who happens along where you can find a blue blouse. The answer, if you're lucky enough to get an honest one, is that there are probably about 20 different places in that store where you can find a blue blouse. There are a myriad of designer departments, where each designer's "collection" of clothes is displayed together, and each department probably has several blue blouses. You'll also find blue blouses in the often bizarrely code-named departments around the store—the "Juniors" department, the "Missy" department, the "Bridge" department, and the "Woman's" department. There is also likely to be some private-label offerings spread out along the way. (Believe it or not, many women actually have learned to understand this Byzantine system, a testament to the intelligence and perseverance of the customer.) This system exists because the store executives and the designers want it that way, not because the customers prefer it.

Department stores also are notorious for their mazelike layouts and for having few, if any, directional signs. Do you have to walk the entire length of the floor to find an escalator to bring you to the next floor? That's because department store operators, who ruled the retail roost for several decades, wanted customers to become lost in their stores. The thinking is that a lost customer must spend more time in the store, and may eventually stumble into something to buy. The store's interest is put ahead of the customer's interest.

Department stores are hardly the only offenders. Walk into a supermarket and ask a sales associate (if you can find one) where the pizza is located. As in our department store example, there's probably pizza in at least four different sections of that supermarket. You'll find pizza in the deli, in the refrigerated aisle, in the meat department, and in the frozen food aisle. The better supermarkets may even have some hot and ready to sell by the slice or the whole pie. Why would one product be sold in so many places? Because that's how the chain (and its various buying departments) buys pizza, not because of any sophisticated research that suggests the customer wants to search four or five different departments.

Let's say that in addition to pizza your grocery list includes eggs and milk, some of the more frequently consumed items a customer purchases. We'd wager that 9.9 times out of 10, you're going to have to walk to the far back of that store, because that's where nearly all supermarkets keep staples like eggs and milk. Again, the supermarket operator is looking to keep you in that store as long as possible, with the hope that you'll buy more stuff. It is also probably close to where the product was delivered into the store and the most convenient place to build refrigerated cases. Again, the retailer's interest is put ahead of the customer's interest.

In just about every category of retail you can think of, these little tricks are designed for the store's profit and convenience, not the customer's. This is not a tell-all book on retailer tricks of the trade, but we offer a few examples to debunk the myth that retailers put customers first.

In many cases, retailers are forced to rely on these tricks because their basic proposition to the customer is broken: The only way to make a profit is to trick the customer into buying items they might not need. As we discuss in later chapters, we are not against the more pragmatic elements of retail success. In fact, we readily acknowledge that a retailer must make difficult decisions to develop a profitable model. We just want to make sure that the reasons retailers act are stated up front, not as part of the grand notion of "acting on behalf of the customer."

**Myth 2:**   Retailers understand customer service.
**Reality:**   Customers know better.

We have been deeply involved with conducting, analyzing, and understanding customer research on behalf of our clients throughout the nearly 18 years of our practice (and our partners headed research practices internally for retailers an additional 20 years before that). We estimate that we have seen more consumer research, across more categories of products, than just about anyone. We look at dozens of studies and talk to thousands of customers each and every year. One thing has remained constant—customers and retailers have very different notions about customer service.

One of the first questions we ask new clients is to see all of their research they have conducted concerning their customers. The typical answer is perhaps surprising: Too often, very little research has focused specifically on what their customers really think about their store. Sure, there may be the odd tracking study, advertising awareness survey, or focus group, but few retailers take the time to extensively study their own customers. We often hear the same phrase: "We know what our customers want—we don't need research." Wrong again.

When retailers are asked to define great customer service, they almost always say something about having wonderful people. Historically, customer service has been equated with people: hand-holding, smiling, greeting shoppers, and, of course, heavy doses of "yes ma'am, yes sir, thank-you-very-much-and-have-a-nice-day."

# Customers Are #1

Customers, too, think genuine customer service and courtesy are great. They would love to experience that on a more regular basis. However, for them, it's the *fourth* most important aspect of customer service. Surprised? So are most retailers.

Here are the top four reasons given by customers when they're asked to define great customer service:

1. Having the product they are looking for that solves their needs—and having it in stock. Simply put: Sell what I need and actually have it on the shelf when I come to the store.
2. Having a store that is logically laid out so customers can find what they want without wasting their time. This includes easy entrance to and exit from the parking lot, readily available parking, baskets available, and shopping carts that actually work. It also includes the basics of navigation (way-finding in retailspeak). This includes logical adjacencies of products, clear signage, and clearly marked products. Finally, it includes customer public enemy number 1—the checkout lines. They need to be staffed and moving fast—or perhaps in the future, eliminated altogether.
3. Having information readily available to answer questions and to help the customer decide what to buy—either signs, brochures, or salespeople. Provide the tools customers need to help make intelligent buying decisions in the store.
4. Finally, it is important to have friendly, knowledgeable people. While many retailers equate great customer service with great people, customers equate great customer service with things that make shopping easier and more efficient. Having great people is just one part of that.

This is a critical misunderstanding for retailers, because it creates an unrealistic, even mythical expectation. If customer service were actually dependent on having wonderful sales associates who had the

27

magical ability to sense and respond to each customer's whim and mood, how could retailers go about creating a system to ensure that happens? It would be extraordinarily difficult, and most certainly couldn't afford it. Unfortunately, many try and fail.

Few retailers are given credit for having wonderful customer service, partly because too many are chasing an unattainable nirvana. It would be like trying to find a spouse who could read your mind and understand your every whim and mood. Wonderful, perhaps; realistic, probably not.

Many retailers are busy trying to find and cultivate those mythical, mind-reading salespeople (all in a way that doesn't cost too much money, of course) instead of developing non-people-related processes that enhance customer service from the customer's perspective.

The good news here is that customers have realistic expectations. They don't demand mind-reading salespeople—they know such a thing isn't possible. Customers merely want the item they're looking for to be in stock. They want information, from a salesperson, a sign or a brochure, and they want to be able to find their way around the store easily. Retailers that are successful in delivering these three things rate well with customers. If the stores also have knowledgeable and friendly people, that's gravy.

> **Myth 3:** Retailers understand who their customers are.
> **Reality:** Customers have changed dramatically over the past couple decades, and many retailers haven't changed with them.

There was a time when targeting customers was a relatively easy proposition. Target the baby boomers, ages 25 to 44, who were in the process of having families, buying cars and homes, and accumulating a lot of material possessions. From the 1950s to the 1970s, those customers were also likely to look a lot alike: They were

Caucasians who defined the broad middle class of the United States and had similar family composition and makeup—the standard 2.6 kids, a wife who stayed home, a station wagon, dog, and house in the suburbs. The profile of the U.S. consumer has changed dramatically; unfortunately, our retailers have not.

Let's start with income. The media wrote much in the late 1990s about the nation's prosperity and about the longest bull market in history that inflated the nation's 401(k)s, whetting our collective appetites for pricey baubles, fancy imported cars, and other luxuries. A barely noted sidebar, however, is the fact that for the vast majority of Americans, the past two decades weren't all that prosperous. (See Figure 2.1.)

The wealthiest 20 percent of Americans saw their mean household income increase 49 percent (in constant dollars) from 1980 to 2001—that's almost five times the gains made by the rest of the population. Over the same 20 years, the nation's poorest quintile saw its income increase only 4 percent, to $10,136, while the middle quintile (third wealthiest, third poorest) saw its income rise 11 percent, to $42,629.

**FIGURE 2.1**   Mean Household Income by Quintile

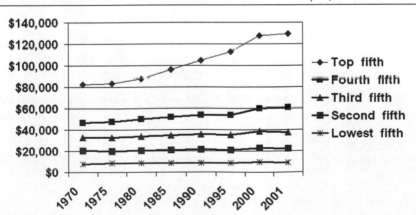

While the rich got richer, a great majority of the population saw very modest gains in their buying power over the past two decades. It has polarized our society into haves and have-nots. Not surprisingly, that has made the many have-nots increasingly value-driven, which helped propel Wal-Mart to the top spot as the nation's largest retailer and the nation's largest company. It has also served to shrink the so-called middle, which has been the foundation of most retailers' strategies for the past century. Retailers simply chose to place their offer at the center of society's demographics in terms of age and income. The center is no longer so easy to pinpoint and is increasingly less relevant.

It's well known that America's population is older now than it has ever been. In 1980 there were approximately 60 million people over 50 years of age. Today that number is approaching 100 million, or roughly one-third of the population. (See Figure 2.2.) Despite

**FIGURE 2.2**   Percent of Population over 50

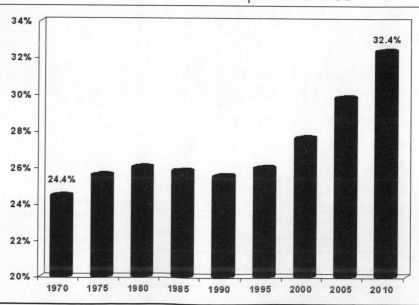

our efforts to conceal it—from wrinkle-hiding Botox injections to performance-enhancing pharmaceuticals like Viagra—we're still getting older. While the nation's supermarkets, drugstores, and malls are already crammed with products that cater to the aging population, graying baby boomers present additional challenges for retailers.

Today's boomers are hardly acting like the older consumers of past generations, and their desire to be in control will place immense pressures on retailers. Older customers are experienced shoppers who have previously bought numerous TVs, cars, and homes. Because they are seasoned shoppers, they tend to be more demanding shoppers. They demand the best they can get for their money and a no-nonsense sales approach.

America also has fewer so-called traditional families—those in which one parent works (typically the father) and the mother is a full-time homemaker. (See Figure 2.3.) In 1950, such families accounted for more than 60 percent of the U.S. labor force. Today they make up less than 15 percent, just barely ahead of single-parent families headed by a working mother. Two-income families now

**FIGURE 2.3**  Traditional Family in Decline

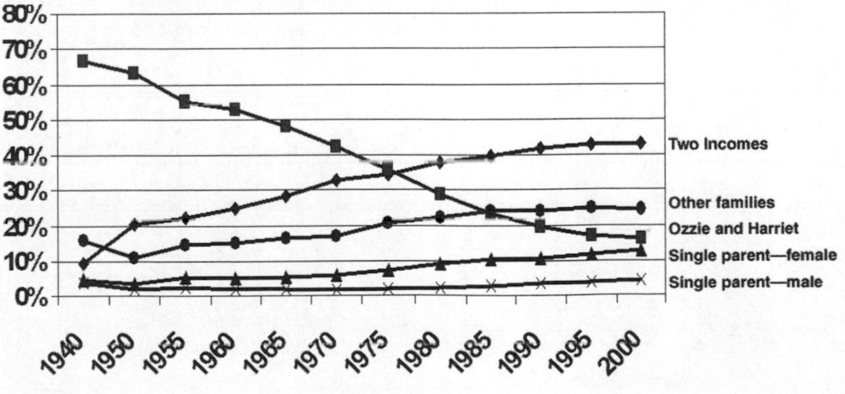

make up more than 40 percent of the labor force, more than double the percentage in 1950.

We like to tell retailers: Ozzie and Harriet don't live here anymore. (See Figure 2.4.) It's an important message, because many retail stores were established to serve people like Ozzie and Harriet, the title characters of a popular 1950s sitcom that portrayed traditional family life in suburbia. Today, many retailers are still trying to serve this customer base, even though it's not there anymore. (Perhaps that's because many retail executives still live in Ozzie-and-Harriet-type households.) In fact, today's nuclear family looks a little bit like the Ozzy Osbourne family that has captivated reality television. This is hardly the same vision of America.

One reason these customers aren't around anymore is because Harriet now works outside the home. Only 36.7 percent of women

**FIGURE 2.4**   Ozzie and Harriet Don't Live Here Anymore . . .
but Ozzy Does!

© Corbis                              © Corbis

ages 20 to 64 were in the workforce in 1950. The Bureau of Labor Statistics predicts that by 2005 75.2 percent of women in that age group will hold down jobs. Amazingly, few retailers have yet to adequately address the needs of working women. (See Figure 2.5.)

Finally, Americans are more ethnically diverse. (See Figure 2.6.) We're still the melting pot, but it's no longer a European-based mixture. By 2010, Hispanics, Asians, and blacks will account for nearly 33 percent of the country's population. In 1980, that figure stood at 19.7 percent. Retailers are far behind consumer product manufacturers and other industries in realizing the increasing importance of ethnic customers. At the same time, the general public's taste for ethnic-inspired products and services has increased and will continue to do so. Our tastes in food, music, and fashion have already changed dramatically as a result of the increasing ethnic influences on society.

**FIGURE 2.5**   Women in the Workforce

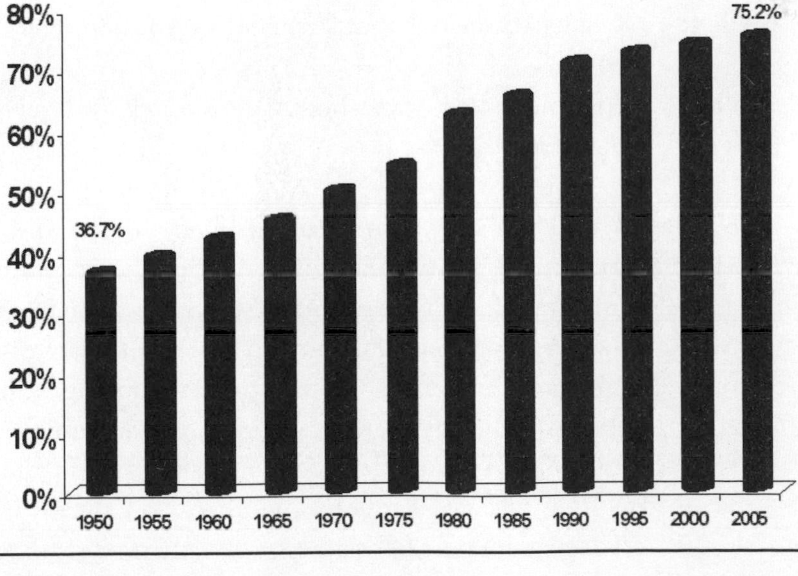

**FIGURE 2.6** Exploding Ethnic Population

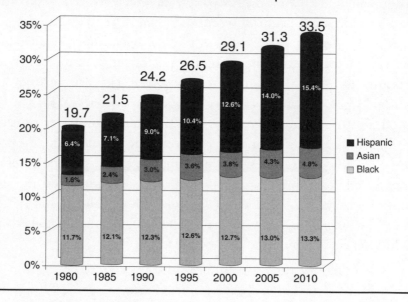

Ethnics as a Percent of Total Population

**Myth 4:** Retailers believe that customers love to shop their stores.

**Reality:** Customers don't love shopping—most don't even like shopping.

The store is well lit. The floors sparkle. The merchandise is stacked immaculately and looks inviting. The Muzak is at just the right level. The motivated, well-trained sales staff is ready and eager to please. To a retailer, it's a beautiful thing. What's not to love?

Plenty. To the great majority of consumers, shopping is just another chore—slightly more enjoyable than, say, vacuuming or cleaning the house. Many consumers today view shopping as a hassle and a headache. While good retailers agonize over details that improve customers' shopping experiences, customers are far less committed and involved with the experience. They just want to find what they're looking for and then get back to more important matters in their lives.

As our national profile has evolved over the past few decades, several troubling trends for retailers have emerged about the way consumers view shopping. Consumers increasingly see shopping as a hassle that eats up precious free time, and they want to spend less time shopping. Remember that two-income households are the norm today. In a survey of such families, 71 percent said they do their shopping on weekends. And nearly 9 out of 10 of them reported that they would like to spend less time shopping. While shopping was once America's unofficial national pastime, consumers now have a bewildering array of choices vying for increasingly shrinking free time. Necessity shopping can be a tedious chore; leisure-time shopping is also scarce.

It's a trend that has hurt malls around the country. In 1980, people visited malls 3.1 times per month. In 2000, shoppers went to the mall only 1.6 times per month. Even more telling, in 1980 shoppers spent 10 hours per month at a mall. By 2000, that figure had plummeted to 3.5 hours. These figures include a large number of the population who never even go to malls.

Consumers shop less often than they did 10 years ago, and they want to shop even less. Today, customers are more selective about where they shop, often taking a destination-shopping approach rather than browsing at several different stores. They go to their first or second choice and that's it.

Today's customers also are increasingly value-driven, partly due to the nominal gains in buying power for most Americans over the past two decades. In 1989, Americans spent more money in department stores than they did at discount stores. Ten years later, Americans spent three times as much at discount stores as they did at department stores. Of course, discount stores expanded far more rapidly in the 1990s than did the mature department store industry. We believe that a significant factor was an evolving customer

35

perception. Over those years, shoppers came to see discount stores as synonymous with value. At the same time, they came to see department stores as having inflated prices and as being too time-consuming and unwieldy to shop.

Consumers are shopping at places that they believe offer the best value as they look to stretch their tight budgets. They're also looking for low prices on familiar brands—so they don't have to spend time worrying about whether the merchandise quality is up to snuff.

Finally, consumers simply have far more choices about where they shop than they did even 10 or 20 years ago. When shopping for commodity-driven products, consumers had little choice in where they would buy goods. Sure, they could switch from one local grocery chain to another, but they couldn't abandon the format altogether. Even today, supermarkets enjoy 100 percent shopper penetration, but those customers are coming less often; they are now able to buy frequently used consumer food and household products at a growing number of formats. (See Figure 2.7.)

No retailer can assume customers love shopping their stores. Nor can they assume that the customer really doesn't have a choice.

**Myth 5:** Retailers believe they can successfully control customers.

**Reality:** Customers have too many options and will go elsewhere if forced to do it the retailer's way.

To thrive in the future, retailers must truly become customer-centric. That means putting customers in control. We believe putting customers in control is the future of customer service and the future of retailing as well. It involves finally giving customers control of the shopping and buying process.

After centuries of being in control, today's retailers find this notion frightening. How can retailers relinquish control and make their traditional profit formulas work at the same time?

**FIGURE 2.7**   Grocery Stores Losing Shoppers
to Competing Channels

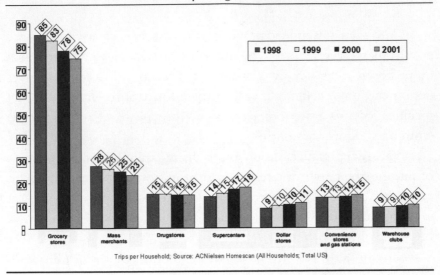

Trips per Household; Source: ACNielsen Homescan (All Households; Total US)

There are many ways to put customers in control:

- Give them the ability to shop and buy any way they please: from a catalog by phone, from a web site by computer or handheld PDA, or in a store.
- Make it easy for them to find what they're looking for at your store. Remove elements of your store that cause customers problems or waste their time—even if that means passing up sales opportunities.
- Make product information readily available so they can easily make informed decisions.
- Provide a sales process that lets them decide whether they want to browse on their own or talk with a salesperson.
- Allow them to handle checkout by themselves.
- Provide a seamless shopping experience from store to catalog to web site.

- Put stores where customers are—in airports, offices, grocery stores, suburbia, or inner-cities.

If knowledge is indeed power, then customers clearly have more power than ever before. The Internet provides something much more potent than simply a channel for remote shopping. It gives customers unprecedented access to information—from product specifications to price comparisons. More power has heightened customers' desire for control.

That's why retailers simply must change their long-held practice of putting their own interests ahead of customers' interests. That's easier said than done, however. Anybody in retail who claims that it isn't an issue for his or her company is either ignorant or wearing a snug pair of reality blinders.

The modern era of retail, which began in the 1930s with the emergence of mass merchants like Sears and J.C. Penney, has focused on achieving efficiencies of scale so retailers could deliver more products faster and cheaper. The main driving forces were lower operating costs, lower prices for consumers, and more productive stores. That has meant greater profits and growth for retailers. For customers, the chief benefits have been large selection and low prices. The trade-offs—and customers accepted these willingly—have been less-specialized service and fewer professional sales associates. Additionally, customers have had to endure merchandising schemes and store layouts that favor the retailer rather than the customer.

Today, having competitive prices and assortments only gets a retailer into the game. The story of tomorrow's winning retailers will be customer control and customer efficiency. When customers are asked in focus groups what they're looking for in a store, historically the top responses have been quality products, fair prices, and good service. Now customers say that time is equally important. Customers are looking for stores that can service them quickly, without wasting their precious time. The only way retailers can do this is to develop stores and processes that are efficient for customers and that put customers in control.

Customers today don't go shopping—they go buying. They "burst-shop," making shorter trips and visiting fewer stores. They won't come back to a store that wastes their time or has only some of what they need—thereby forcing them to make another trip. Bottom line for retailers: Customers are vacating the middle. They no longer go to three or four stores before buying. That's why stores that are third or fourth best are in peril. That's why being a pretty good store, or anything less than the best, isn't good enough anymore.

Putting the customer first will become a reality for today's retailers. The faster they adapt their practices, the better chance they have of surviving into the future.

# PART II
# The Practice

# CHAPTER THREE

# CHEAP-EST: WINNING WITH PRICE

Let's dive into exactly what we mean by an Est-driven strategy. Retailers who pursue a particular Est don't do so to the exclusion of other attributes of their business. On the contrary, they can't afford to lose sights of the other drivers of retail success. What they are successful at, however, is taking one key attribute and making it the cornerstone of their strategy, understood by consumers and associates alike.

In the following chapters, we outline exactly what each of the Ests means, and we provide examples of retailers who win by pursuing that path. For good measure, we also include their growth over a historical period of time to prove that Est also pays off on the bottom line.

## CHEAP-EST DEFINED

Cheap-Est means consistently having lower prices than the competition on the products that a retailer sells. It is a straightforward and easily understood proposition, the most basic of the Est concepts to grasp. It is also an extremely valuable proposition for consumers, especially considering that many Americans have had only small gains in their buying power over the past two decades.

Even affluent consumers appreciate bargains, which explains why Cheap-Est retailers have the opportunity for huge sales volumes. Wal-Mart, the quintessential Cheap-Est retailer, is now the world's largest company—bigger than conglomerates like Exxon and General Electric.

Yet being Cheap-Est requires tremendous discipline and operational excellence. It is also very difficult for multiple retailers to occupy the Cheap-Est positioning—you're either low-priced or you're not. In some ways, Cheap-Est has less margin of error than any other Est position.

Before we begin, let's have a necessary semantics discussion about often used and abused words in consumer marketing—*cheap* and *value*. Some retail executives bristle at the word *cheap*. They think (and in many instances are correct) that cheap means bad quality. But cheap is a word customers use (approvingly) to talk about low prices. For good measure, Merriam-Webster defines *cheap* as "purchasable below the going price or the real value" or "charging or obtainable at a low price." Retailers should get used to the word. That's how customers talk, so that's how retailers should talk.

The favorite word (and strategy) of non-Est retailers has to be *value*. As in, "We provide a great value to our customers." In fact, we have to work hard to avoid this word in our writings as well. It is easy to fall into the trap of creating a value proposition for the consumer. While this is not wrong (and value is critical), it is vital to look into the individual elements that create value. If your value is simply a summing up of many "pretty goods," you're headed for the Black Hole. A sustainable value proposition better have an Est or it is not very valuable at all. Value is the great weasel word of the retail and supplier world—it does not, however, make you a success.

# Cheap-Est: Winning with Price

All retailers believe they provide value. Everyone from Neiman Marcus (high prices, exclusive products, highly personalized service) to Dollar General (low prices, limited assortments, limited service) will say they provide value. Est is the essence of that value equation. In the case of Dollar General, a genuine Est—cheapest prices—is driving its value equation. Neiman Marcus can claim Easy-Est to its exclusive cadre of customers. Both can talk value, but it is the Est driver of the formula that is the key. If you say you provide value, prove it.

To be best on price, stores must singularly devote themselves to being the low-cost operator. We think of low operating costs as the Siamese twin of low prices. You cannot be Cheap-Est if your costs of running the business are higher than your competitors. If you try, your competitors will undercut your prices and eventually drive you out of business. Having low prices on the front end—the shelves—demands low costs on the back end.

In addition to buying smart, shipping inexpensively, controlling inventory, operating low-rent, low-cost stores, having an efficient supply chain, and arranging merchandise in the stores with as little cost as possible, Cheap-Est retailers must do the little things, like counting rubber bands and paper clips. They must create a pervasive culture throughout the company that every penny is critical—because, in fact, it is. Cheap-Est retailers understand that their entire organization must embrace the culture of low prices and low costs.

Other Est positions can cover a lot of sins. For instance, if a store is Hot-Est, it can be sloppy in some operating areas and customers will still come. If a store has locational dominance and is Quick-Est for lots of shoppers, it can win until someone figures out a way to overcome that advantage. However, if a retailer attempting to be Cheap-Est loses its cost advantage and must either raise prices or give up profits to maintain its low prices, the retailer will eventually lose. Or it will be forced to pursue a different Est position.

Part of the genius of Wal-Mart was that Sam Walton viewed his operation from a distribution perspective rather than from a store perspective. He understood that taking costs and inefficiencies out of the supply chain was critical to opening stores that could win at being Cheap-Est. Wal-Mart's core purpose was always low prices. Its core operational mission has always been low costs. It was a mission personified by Sam Walton, driving to stores in his beat-up old pickup truck. It's why Wal-Mart is often criticized for it ruthless demands on vendors for rock-bottom prices. Having low prices is everything to Wal-Mart, and in turn, so is having low costs.

A company must have an ingrained low-cost culture to even attempt to be Cheap-Est. If executives and middle management can't live without some of the perks and niceties of other companies, Cheap-Est probably isn't an option. This may sound rather simplistic, but we've found that a company's culture is a key driver of Cheap-Est success: Usually, you need only pull up to a retail headquarter's front doors or peak into a CEO's office: If it is posh and opulent, watch out—low costs aren't part of the culture. Wal-Mart runs the world's largest company in unassuming headquarters in an unassuming town.

Retailers also must assess the competition and be realistic about their chances of bringing their operating costs below the costs of their competitors. If someone else occupies that position, a direct assault typically doesn't work. Yet we are amazed at the constant innovation that has occurred historically in retailing to get costs out of the system and find new ways to deliver low prices to consumers.

Wal-Mart, of course, has made it tough for most other retailers to stake their claim as Cheap-Est. Still, there are some exceptions, and we examine one, Costco, in the following pages. In addition to Wal-Mart, other Cheap-Est retailers include Dollar General, Fred's, Family Dollar, Trader Joe's, and Costco. The beauty (and fun) of retailing lies in the continuing ability to figure out a way to undercut the incumbent. If Wal–Mart is the $200 billion gorilla, there is still a way for other retailers to undercut the company on costs—as long as they recognize the key Est principle of sacrificing one element to provide another.

In fact, we are incredibly intrigued by eBay, which we believe is the real revolutionary development in e-commerce. eBay (mostly mom-and-pop merchants and people operating out of their garages and basements) is already making strides toward becoming the new Cheap-Est proponent. As ruthlessly efficient and effective as Wal–Mart can be, can they compete against people selling products directly from their homes with almost no overhead? By sacrificing almost all of the costs associated with running a retail enterprise (real estate, employees, etc.), eBay may truly usher in the next generation of Cheap-Est operators. (See Figure 3.1.)

**FIGURE 3.1**    Est Chart: Cheap-Est Retailers

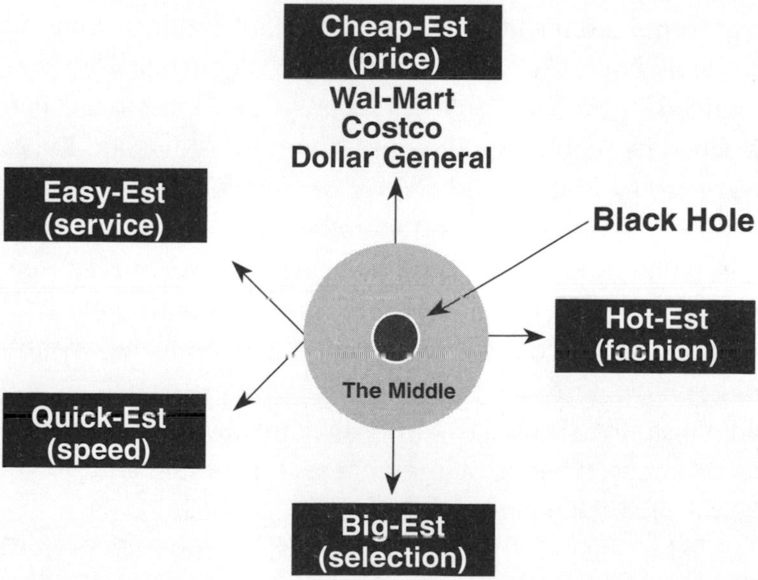

## Cheap-Est: Costco

The story of Costco, the nation's largest chain of warehouse club stores, begins in 1976, when a man named Sol Price founded the eponymous and appropriately named Price Club. With Price Club, Sol Price pioneered a new breed of retailers—warehouse clubs.

Many industry observers scratched their heads over his experiment and are still doing so today because of the enduring success of warehouse clubs like Costco, which was cofounded in 1983 by a former Price Club executive named Jim Sinegal. The two chains merged in 1993, and in 2003 Costco produced a staggering $42 billion in sales at 420 stores in seven countries. Each Costco store, on average, produces $100 million a year in sales, a volume that's unmatched by any of Costco's competitors and represents the largest average store volumes of any retailer, period. It's also a powerful testament to Costco's popularity with customers.

Still, Price Club blazed the trail. When the store was founded in the late 1970s, it seemed that mass retail had reached its zenith—the discount stores. Wal-Mart and Kmart were stores that embodied the driving forces behind the modern era of retail: lower operating costs, lower prices for consumers, and more productive stores. Still today, few retailers other than warehouse clubs can consistently beat Wal-Mart in these areas. Wal-Mart is lauded as the world's most efficient retailer. Yet Wal-Mart has selling, general, and administrative (SG&A) expenses that are about 16 percent of its revenues, while Costco manages to maintain a far lower SG&A of about 9 percent.

To be Cheap-Est, which means best on price, stores must devote themselves to being the low-cost operator. Costco epitomizes this with unflinching devotion. Costco is a great case study because it achieved an Est position and then lever-aged that position to expand its purpose and become even better for its select group of customers.

Costco has been the most creative and consistent retailer in executing the warehouse club format. Clubs look decep-tively simple to operate and seem very easy to copy. In fact, Price Club spawned a dozen imitators (including one from McMillan|Doolittle founder Sid Doolittle), and even today it is physically difficult to tell one club store apart from another. But, Costco, with its superior execution, easily outperforms them all. Because Costco delivers time and again for cus-tomers, those customers have come to think of Costco as their trusted purchasing agent. That essentially gives Costco license to sell just about anything, because its customers trust Costco to deliver great products and services at the lowest price.

Before we discuss how Costco became a winner, let's talk about the warehouse club format and what made Price Club so revolutionary. To become Cheap-Est, warehouse clubs shattered nearly every retail convention.

- For starters, Price Club limited its customer base to business owners who were willing to pay an annual membership fee. Other consumers were not welcome—despite the retail convention that says stores should attract more people, not fewer. Cus-tomers were literally turned away from the doors—imagine that!
- Price Club didn't advertise special sales. It didn't have loss leaders and products with high markups—despite standard wisdom that says retail is all about maximiz-ing margins on certain items. If Price Club couldn't beat a conventional retailer's price, it simply wouldn't sell the item.

- In fact, Price Club didn't advertise at all, even though almost all other retailers rely heavily on ads to get consumers through the door. It didn't even accept credit cards, despite the fact that customer order sizes were quite large by dollar amount.
- Price Club sold products in large, bulky quantities—despite retail convention that says products should be broken into small quantities so that more people will buy them.

Sol Price chose to shatter these and other retail tenets because he wanted Price Club to have a sharp focus: to be Cheap-Est for customers who can afford to stock up. Sol Price was betting that customers—business owners and eventually individuals who could afford to buy in bulk—would accept these trade-offs in return for getting tremendous bargains. He made the quintessential Est decision: Be best for only certain customers. The corollary, and the part where most retailers fail, is that retailers must be willing to accept what we call the "intelligent loss of sales."

- Warehouse clubs aren't a value to consumers who are buying a $1 bottle of ketchup at a dollar store because they have only $50 in their checking account.
- Warehouse clubs aren't designed to be easy or quick to shop for small families and single apartment dwellers who might spend $25 a week there.

In fact, that's where other warehouse clubs ran into trouble. Many operators strayed from their core proposition to try to appeal to these shoppers and wound up with the smaller buyers clogging the checkout lines at the expense of the big spenders. In turn, their stores became less productive.

# Cheap-Est: Winning with Price

Warehouse clubs are Cheap-Est because their operating costs are lowest. They operate bare-bones warehouse stores. They don't advertise. They stock a small number of SKUs (different products, known in retail as stockkeeping units). Costco stores have about 3,500 SKUs, whereas supermarkets have about 35,000, and discount stores have about 100,000. That results in volume discounts, but it also means Costco achieves high inventory turnover and handles significantly fewer items (mostly on pallets).

Most products are shipped to Costco from the manufacturer ready to be put on the sales floor. That's a tremendous saving on labor costs—Costco doesn't have to unbox, unbundle, and arrange items on its shelves.

While the membership fee generates revenue, it also has a cost-savings role because it reduces *shrink,* which is retail-speak for shoplifting. Most stores write off about 1.5 percent of their sales every year to shrink. Costco has that down to 0.04 percent. Based on its $42 billion sales in fiscal 2002, that's an annual savings of nearly $500 million.

In Costco's 2001 annual report—which has no color photos and features the same cover as the previous three years (only the dates change)—Costco chairman Jeff Brotman and CEO Jim Sinegal write: "We always consider expense control to be our biggest challenge. . . . Our shareholders can be certain that we are committed to evaluating and challenging expenses throughout the company, and bringing these cost savings to the bottom line." The letter also mentions an energy conservation initiative that led to a 15 percent companywide reduction in energy consumption. Costco isn't cutting its energy use to become "greener." Costco is looking to become leaner. That's the type of dedication to low costs required to succeed at Cheap-Est.

What set Costco apart from its current peers—Wal-Mart,

Sam's Club, and BJ's Wholesale Club—is that from its inception Costco incorporated upscale merchandise. Costco realizes that business owners keep their personal credit card in the same wallet with their corporate credit card. That's why Costco sells cashmere sweaters, espresso machines, high-priced patio furniture, and $40,000 diamonds. That's also why Costco shoppers—who may be there to stock up on computer paper and printer cartridges—can find seafood and artisan breads as well as products from exclusive vendors like Titleist, Thomasville, and Elizabeth Arden. In fact, Costco is now the nation's largest seller of wine—those business customers turned out to be pretty good consumers as well.

Business owners are perfect personal consumers for Costco because they tend to be affluent and value-driven (even frugal) shoppers who love the hunt and the thrill of a bargain. The additional benefit for Costco has been that other affluent consumers flock to Costco thanks to word of mouth. It's similar to Home Depot's attraction: Many people want to shop at Home Depot because it's where the professionals (the contractors) shop. In some regards, business owners are professional consumers. Other consumers want to join the club—and shop where the pros shop.

Costco also has built up a great amount of integrity by staying true to its low-margin approach and refusing to sell items that can't offer a demonstrable value. For instance, for years Costco didn't sell diapers. Why? Because other retailers sell diapers as loss leaders, so Costco couldn't provide a good value. Today Costco sells its own private-label diapers. Sure, Costco missed out on selling plenty of diapers over the years. However, it was an intelligent loss of sales, because selling diapers at the same price charged by discounters or supermarkets would diminish Costco's position as Cheap-Est.

In that case, making a sale in the short term could hurt over the long term. It's a tough decision to make, but it's the kind of discipline it takes to be an Est retailer.

Costco communicates its value proposition to customers in many small but important ways. A great example is in food service. Costco sells a hot dog and soda for $1.50 at its in-store restaurants, a price that hasn't changed in years. Costco could charge more and customers wouldn't blink. However, it's a symbolic statement about commitment to the lowest price, and it's a meaningful one to customers—who buy something like 40 million hot dogs a year at Costco.

Costco also has internal policies that emphasize low prices. For instance, Sinegal requires a written request for his personal approval before any item is marked up more than 18 percent above cost. Sinegal says he has never given such approval. In fact, he's never seen such a request.

It is a nearly irresistible temptation for retailers to pass on higher costs to the consumer or simply to take whatever margins the marketplace will allow. This is the way most retailers work and think—looking to maximize margins to increase profitability. Not Costco. Even in the mid-1990s, at the height of the rage over Beanie Babies, Costco stuck to its policy of not taking more from the consumer. It had the lowest prices just about anywhere on the bean-filled stuffed animals that were selling for three to four times suggested retail at many stores. The short-term profit potential was too great for some merchants to pass up, but Costco stayed true to its philosophy. While Beanie Baby mania eventually died (thankfully), customers' perception of Costco as a low-price leader lives on.

In fact, Costco is willing to do the unthinkable—risk the wrath of Wall Street to stay true to its customers. In the second quarter of 2003, Costco announced lower earnings and lower projected future earnings for the remainder of the year, despite the fact that its sales continue to remain robust. Two reasons were given to shareholders: One was the rising cost of employee benefits, particularly in California, where Costco has a significant store base. The second was that the company is fighting Sam's (Wal-Mart) on low prices. This is intriguing because consumers typically don't shop from club to club. Another company would have been tempted to "manage to the quarter" and not disappoint Wall Street, and Costco's stock did take a significant short-term hit. Still, the company stuck resolutely to its core principle of Cheap-Est. While it may have cost Costco on the stock market, it is clear that the company is continuing to win the hearts and wallets of consumers.

The future remains very bright for this Est retailer. It has been able to successfully leverage its position as the customer's trusted purchasing agent into new product and service categories, from gasoline and hearing aids to business-related services. Costco has continually expanded its fresh food offerings to add from-scratch bakeries and prime meats. Finally, it has been able to introduce private-label products into its stores under the Kirkland banner. Again, however, Costco has emphasized quality over margin and built up its brand equity by providing the consumer with exceptional product at an exceptional price.

Costco has continually outpaced the entire retail industry on key measures of productivity. It is also outpacing retailers on comparable store sales, an even more important measure of its ability to continually win over consumers to its low-cost, low price format.

Costco remains one of our favorite retailers for its unflinching commitment to its Est principle. (See Table 3.1.)

**TABLE 3.1**   Performance of Cheap-Est Retailer: Costco

|  | 1993 Fiscal Year | 2002 Fiscal Year | Increase (%), 1993–2002 |
|---|---|---|---|
| Net sales ($ millions) | $15,155 | $41,690 | 11 |
| Net income ($ millions) | $223 | $721 | 13 |
| Operating profit (%) | 2.4 | 2.7 | N/A |
| Number of stores | 200 | 420 | 7.8 |

Note: Costco's fiscal year ends in August.

AVOIDING THE BLACK HOLE

# KMART

Kmart pioneered the discount retail format. It came up with the great idea to eliminate service elements and other cost centers of department stores to sell products cheaper. This made Kmart one of the most successful and fastest-growing retailers in history. Its downfall was in not keeping up with competitors—Est positions don't last forever.

From its humble origins in Bentonville, Arkansas, Wal-Mart quietly began opening stores in small rural towns that had been all but ignored by other retailers. At the outset, Sam Walton certainly didn't have the buying power and muscle of mighty Kmart, but he figured out ways to beat the giant at its own game.

Wal-Mart won on execution as well, by making sure that the stores stayed stocked and that the store employees had a vested interest in its success. Wal-Mart was an early pioneer of profit sharing, and there are legions of stories about Wal-Mart truck drivers and store clerks who retired as millionaires.

Kmart lost its standing as Cheap-Est, yet over the years it developed no new reason to attract customers. Kmart simply couldn't win at Cheap-Est because Wal-Mart, with its relentless drive to lower costs, had developed a far lower cost structure than Kmart's. Meanwhile, another competitor, Target, figured out how to incorporate more fashionable merchandise in a discount store.

What had once made Kmart great—offering a huge amount of low-price, low-quality merchandise for sale in a no-frills self-help setting—was no longer sufficient. Customers had better options, and Kmart had become second-tier by 1988, when Dustin Hoffman's character hissed "Kmart sucks" in the movie *Rain Man.*

Wal-Mart spent heavily on technology related to its distribution. It pioneered technology that enabled stores to communicate sales data instantly—helping them to run more efficiently and do a better job of keeping stores in stock. Rather than taking a distribution approach, Kmart took a store approach. It built stores to increase its sales—and would later worry about building distribution centers to support its stores. Naturally, that led to higher costs and more inefficient systems. At one point, Kmart admitted its in-stock position was only 70 percent. That means 3 times out of 10, customers could not find the product they were looking for. We know that having products in stock is one of the most important things to customers, which meant Kmart was literally sending unsatisfied customers to its competitors.

Wal-Mart also gained a cost advantage over Kmart by adopting its Everyday Low Prices approach. Kmart, on the other hand, is what's known as a *high-low* operator. That means Kmart prices some items extremely low—and pushes those products by advertising the sales in newspaper inserts—while it sells other items at higher prices with fatter margins.

# Cheap-Est: Winning with Price

This requires Kmart to spend more heavily on advertising. Being a high-low operator also requires Kmart to manage fast-moving inventory, the special promotional items, and slow-moving "museum inventory."

We don't necessarily advocate one pricing approach over another. From a customer perspective, both are fine. High-low operators can win at Cheap-Est, and many retailers have perfected the strategy, but Wal-Mart leveraged the approach to gain an edge at Cheap-Est because its Everyday Low Prices strategy results in moving inventory more consistently. It requires less advertising and means there is less product changeover—so Wal-Mart doesn't have to spend as much time and money labeling and relabeling, arranging and rearranging. Wal-Mart's selling approach thus becomes another tool for driving down its costs. In fact, Kmart's hasty descent into bankruptcy was spurred by an ill-fated attempt to copy Wal-Mart's everyday-low-price strategy—copying the leader ended in disaster.

Still today, Kmart's massive headquarters in Troy, Michigan, looks and feels like the home office of a big, bureaucratic retail company. Wal-Mart executives, we're told, refer to Kmart's headquarters as the Taj Mahal. Wal-Mart's headquarters, not surprisingly, are spartan.

Of course, Kmart's issues go beyond merely what its competitors did. Kmart still is a very large company, and was once a very profitable one. The real lesson was that Kmart had plenty of time to react. It had time to invest, just as Wal-Mart did, in its infrastructure and, in particular, in state-of-the-art logistics technology—or in reinventing a new Est position (like Kohl's). But Kmart didn't.

While Wal-Mart was accelerating its growth, Kmart pursued a diversification strategy as the parent company of successful category-killer chains: Borders, Sports Authority, and

Builders Square. Some of these were decent investments and arguably a viable strategy. Ultimately, however, while Kmart concentrated on these businesses it neglected its core business. By the time Kmart got out of specialty retailing and tried to refocus on fixing Kmart stores, it was too late to catch up to Wal-Mart and Target. Kmart had sailed too far out into the Sea of Mediocrity.

Kmart reemerged from bankruptcy in April of 2003, a much smaller player than it once was but a still formidable $25 billion retailer. Yet, while it has been given a new financial lease on life, it still has not determined its Est. Unfortunately, for retailers who wait too long, a viable Est position may no longer be attainable.

We wish Kmart and its new team success, but painful experience suggests that the lack of an Est will send the company back to the Black Hole—and the next time will probably be permanent.

## CHAPTER FOUR

# BIG-EST: WINNING WITH DOMINANT ASSORTMENTS

When we talk about Big-Est, people often have the misconception that we are talking about store size. They figure that we mean supercenters like Wal-Mart or Meijer, because these are certainly among the largest retail stores in terms of square feet.

Then again, some people believe we're still discussing department stores, which often have huge footprints. In fact, some of the largest retail spaces around belong to department stores, which, in an earlier era of retail development, built flagship stores that boggle the mind.

No, Wal-Mart does not win by being Big-Est. Nor do the department stores. The second misconception: Big-Est means having the most products for sale. That's closer, but still not correct.

We define Big-Est retailers as stores that offer the most dominant assortment in specific categories of merchandise. They are the so-called category killers, like Home Depot in home improvement, PetsMart in pet food and supplies, Bed Bath & Beyond in housewares, Staples in office supplies, Best Buy in home electronics, Toys "R" Us in toys, and Amazon.com in books. (See Figure 4.1.)

**FIGURE 4.1** Est Chart: Big-Est Retailers

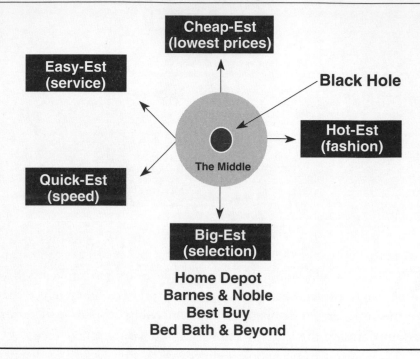

Home Depot
Barnes & Noble
Best Buy
Bed Bath & Beyond

While Big-Est retailers may not have the largest stores in total square feet, they almost always carry the largest selection of products in their category. Toys "R" Us was the first retailer to win on being Big-Est, and in the process it defined a brand-new kind of retailing. Up until the 1970s, generalists—the department stores and mass merchants who carried a little bit of everything—dominated the retail world.

Toys "R" Us changed that, creating a store that became dominant in just a single significant merchandise category. When consumers wanted toys, they thought of Toys "R" Us as the place to go. Toys "R" Us wasn't necessarily the cheapest, and certainly its stores weren't easy to shop, but customers could always count on them to have more to pick from than anyone else. There was great comfort for consumers in the notion that they wouldn't have to shop anyplace else to get their needs met.

The Toys "R" Us formula was quickly copied in just about every imaginable category of merchandise one could think of, including some that bombed. (Do you remember Wedo, the wedding superstore?) The dominant retail trend throughout the 1980s and much of the 1990s was to "category-kill" specific product categories. Needless to say, many of the success stories have become household names.

To win at Big-Est doesn't simply mean having the most merchandise—a mistake some of the less successful formats never fully understood. Big-Est requires being a great merchant. Big-Est retailers must carefully edit their assortments to avoid product overlap as well as products that sell so infrequently it's not economical to carry them. Stocking a store with everything that is available is a disservice to customers because deciding what to buy becomes difficult for them. Larger stores also are more expensive for the retailer to operate, so store productivity and merchandise turnover are critical. Big-Est retailers are constantly paying attention to key productivity measures such as inventory turnover and, more important, gross margin return on investment (GMROI), which balances inventory turnover against how much profit an item can generate.

Two other major considerations for Big-Est merchants are the size of the retail category and the capability and potential for the discount store powerhouses (Wal-Mart and Target) to compete. A retailer's prospects to succeed at Big-Est are enhanced if the category it is pursuing is a large-volume category and if Wal-Mart isn't a serious alternative for shoppers. Home Depot and Lowe's are great examples of Big-Est successes because they compete in the massive $200 billion (plus) home-improvement industry, and discount stores are never going to be able to offer people a comprehensive solution for home-improvement jobs. One investment banker refers to this as the "insulation factor"—how thick the walls are that separate a Wal-Mart or Target from competing in a given category.

The retailers battling it out at pet supply stores, however, struggle with being in a smaller-volume industry. Plus, the battle is more difficult because Wal-Mart and supermarkets can do a fairly decent job of covering the basics. In fact, Wal-Mart is already the largest seller of pet food, and the leading brand of pet food is actually a Wal-Mart private label (Ol' Roy, named for Sam Walton's dog). These stores must make sure that their offer includes more than simply the basics in order to succeed.

In more and more categories, the discount stores have been able to add enough product and achieve enough critical mass to be substantial players in their own right. This has made the challenge for Big-Est retailers even tougher—they not only have to keep an eye on direct competitors, but they also need to compete against stores that have multiple weapons at their disposal.

A key financial concern for Big-Est retailers is inventory management. Finding that sweet spot—between too much and too little merchandise—requires merchandising expertise, and it requires retailers to understand their customers' needs. The costs associated with being the Big-Est and carrying very broad assortments in a line or subline can destroy store profitability. Given the proliferation of brands, styles, sizes, colors, flavors, and so forth, the incremental costs of carrying all the SKUs in a product category can be prohibitive. Why carry all that product when a competitor can simply siphon off the best-sellers?

These inventory-related costs, as well as recent shifts in customer shopping attitudes and purchasing behavior and the emergence of the Internet as a Big-Est retailer candidate, have caused us to reexamine Big-Est as a winning Est position for the future. Is Big-Est still relevant as an Est?

## ARE CATEGORY KILLERS STILL KILLERS?

Many category killers like Toys "R" Us, Sports Authority, Pep Boys, and OfficeMax are facing some degree of financial struggle. They are often unable to grow their top-line sales or have run out of locations to open new stores. Of course, some of their woes stem from poor execution and increased competition. We believe in recent years customers have changed in ways that have made life increasingly difficult for Big-Est retailers.

In today's world, where both parents often work and children take part in numerous activities, many consumers are looking for shopping alternatives that save time. The biggest shift in American retailing in the past two decades has been the onslaught of the traditional discount store and then of the supercenter. Besides low prices (Wal-Mart's primary Est), they have the ability to stock a large percentage of the same merchandise carried by specialists. Because the consumer is shopping these supercenters with increasing frequency, the concept of one-stop shopping is actually being fulfilled.

In category after category, Wal-Mart and Target are taking significant share from their category-killer counterparts by offering selected assortments at lower prices.

Or customers may opt for a small specialty store rather than a category killer. Prices may be higher at a specialty store and selection more focused, but chances are customers will receive more personalized help and have a better shopping experience (in particular, easily finding what they want or need). These specialty stores also have the ability to dominate smaller, niche categories and actually provide better assortment than category killers.

Think of how a golf or camping specialty store compares with a sporting goods category killer, or how Toys "R" Us struggled against Zany Brainy in selling educational toys. We call these types of stores microkillers (or line killers), and their proliferation has hurt the more general category killers who are no longer expert enough merchants to satisfy the more demanding consumer.

Another pressure point on Big-Est retailers is the increasing competition from e-commerce, which obliterates the Big-Est playing field from an assortment standpoint. Amazon.com can easily outdo any retail store when it comes to carrying the biggest assortments. They do it cost-effectively by using central warehouses, as opposed to retailers who must duplicate the offer in every store. Also, online retailers often just carry products in a virtual setting, relying on third-party distributors to actually stock and ship the product. This saves Amazon enormous amounts of money by not having to finance and carry inventory.

Because of inventory productivity issues, shifting consumer shopping patterns, and competition from the Internet, we believe that in most retail categories, a retailer can no longer win by solely being Big-Est. The reality of Est has always been that retailers must own one position—but they also have to be very good at one or more other positions. Toys "R" Us was a success because it was Big-Est, but in its heyday it was also Hot-Est. Who else did it have to compete against? To win at Big-Est today, retailers must strengthen their position in at least one additional Est area—whether that's fashion, price, solution-oriented service, or speed-oriented service.

We contend that Big-Est still belongs on the Est chart, however, because it remains a strategy that can be the foundation for retail success. Being Big-Est is a viable way to differentiate yourself from competitors, and it's also a proposition that plays well with customers. Still, we think tomorrow's successful Big-Est retailers must do two things in addition to offering a dominant assortment:

1. They must be viewed by customers as problem solvers—offering solutions, not just a lot of products.

2. They must be viewed by customers as potential time-savers—offering everything customers need, so they don't have to make multiple trips.

Some Big-Est stores have already begun trying to redefine themselves along these lines. Barnes & Noble started a trend by offering a relaxing lifestyle environment for reading and bringing a date and sipping Starbucks coffee. Office Depot, Toys "R" Us, and PetsMart have been experimenting by offering solution- or lifestyle-based merchandising versus category merchandising. The difference is arranging products based on how people use them rather than on product categories. For instance, instead of a grocery store–like aisle of personal computers next to a row of ink-jet printers, a solution- or lifestyle-based merchandising approach would display these items together in a home-office section, along with other home-office-related products. This makes easier shopping for customers looking to outfit a home office, because it means they can stop at one location instead of having to go down several aisles. It also allows the retailer to develop expertise in those lifestyle/use-oriented departments and gives the retailer a better ability to suggest other lifestyle, use-oriented solutions or services.

The intended result is that customers no longer consider the office supply category-killers store as merely a place for commodities like computer paper, printers, and ink cartridges. Instead, customers think of that office supply store as a place to find solutions for outfitting and organizing their home office and other needs.

PetsMart has accomplished a similar result for pet owners by offering grooming, training, veterinary services, day care, and even a pet hotel. PetsMart stores simply cannot succeed by offering more pet food and supplies—the company is attempting to win by strengthening the emotional bond consumers have with their pets and by becoming the comprehensive authority on pet-related issues.

While discounters can certainly field an adequate product offer, they are unlikely to match category killers on the comprehensiveness of their expertise. Category killers, in every category, must be able to convince customers that they are worth a special trip; Barnes & Noble and PetsMart are good examples of how many Big-Est retailers will evolve in the future.

Two of the most compelling examples of Big-Est today are very well known: Home Depot and Amazon.com. Both win by offering the dominant assortment in one category, and both also have excelled at things that make shopping easier for customers.

## Big-Est: Home Depot versus Lowe's

One of the challenges of writing a book on retailing is that there will never be a guaranteed, enduring example of success. Only customers, and a retailer's ability to respond to their changing needs, will determine that honor. Home Depot would have been as close to a sure thing as we could have predicted, and it was probably the most dominant retailer in the 1990s. The company could do no wrong by just about any measure devised—financial, consumer, or other. (See Table 4.1.)

**TABLE 4.1**  Performance of Big-Est Retailer: Home Depot

|  | 1993 | 2002 | Compound Annual Growth Rate (%), 1993–2002 |
|---|---|---|---|
| Net sales ($ millions) | $9,239 | $58,247 | 23 |
| Net income ($ millions) | $457 | $3,664 | 26 |
| Operating profit (%) | 4.2 | 10 | N/A |
| Number of stores | 264 | 1,523* | 22 |

* Number of stores includes Expo Design Centers.

## Big-Est: Winning with Dominant Assortments

Home Depot's recent woes (probably an overstatement—the company still performs at an extraordinarily high level) serve to demonstrate the tenuous nature of Est. A competitor, Lowe's, which has rapidly improved its strategy at a time when Home Depot let its own slide, is catching up.

While Home Depot is still a Big-Est retailer and obviously dominant, its standards at the store level from a customer service and shopability standpoint have slipped enough to let a competitor through the door. Home Depot, though responding aggressively, is proof that an Est position must be earned every day. There are no sure bets in retail, where a customer's business must be earned on a transaction-by-transaction basis. Size, scale, buying power, and locations can take a retailer only so far.

Home Depot wins at Big-Est by dominating each individual category of home improvement, from plumbing to electrical to paint. If Home Depot merely had the largest selection of home-improvement products, so what? That would be meaningless to the customer who goes there to replace a burned-out refrigerator lightbulb—something that probably happens once every five years. If Home Depot doesn't have the refrigerator bulb, that customer won't be impressed with Home Depot's sprawling square footage and its massive merchandise stacks. What makes Home Depot great, and what makes it successful at Big-Est, is that Home Depot carries that lightbulb—and it will be in stock.

From the outside, Home Depot appeared pretty much identical to Builders Square, a hardware superstore that wound up in the Black Hole. Yet Home Depot's stores did twice the sales volume. Why? Because Home Depot was the superior merchant: It had more of the right products at the right price; it made them available at the right time of year and displayed them in the right part of the store.

To offer the dominant selection within all its departments and make the store an effective seller of these items, Home Depot realized it needed to hire—and pay competitively—experts in specialized departments like plumbing, electrical, and paint. The company basically set out to be a collection of specialty shops, aiming to offer the biggest (and right) selection in all its departments.

Home Depot's buyers and management understand do-it-yourself (DIY) customer needs and how DIY customers shop. They also understand the needs of contractors and home-improvement professionals (plumbers, electricians, etc.), a group that represents a large part of Home Depot's target audience. Home Depot does what great merchants do and what retailers must do to win at Big-Est: It scrutinizes each and every item it sells to determine whether the item provides its target customers with a meaningful and necessary choice. It doesn't add items just for the sake of adding items.

In addition to its Big-Est product offer, Home Depot has always been very good at providing how-to information for its DIY customers via in-store signing and point-of-sale (POS) brochures. The company has also done an acceptable job of providing specialized service. Its employees are known for being helpful, courteous, and knowledgeable. At busy times, an employee is often stationed at the store's entrance to greet customers and direct them to the products they're looking for. Returns are handled in a separate area that's usually well staffed and near the main entrance.

It probably could have been argued several years ago that Home Depot was invincible (and the litany of competitors it sent to the Black Hole—Hechingers, Builders Square, Rickel's, Handy Andy, Home Base—would seem to bear that out). Fortunately for consumers, Lowe's didn't see it that way.

## Big-Est: Winning with Dominant Assortments

Using an Est-like attack, Lowe's determined that Home Depot wasn't serving all customers equally well. While the store was terrific for contractors and serious do-it-yourselfers, it often underserved women, a growing constituent in home-improvement buying decisions. By making its stores brighter and easier to shop, with even higher levels of service, and tailoring its assortments to focus more on the softer side of home improvement, Lowe's has been able to more than hold its own against Home Depot in similar markets. This is a terrific example of Est at work.

## Big-Est: Amazon.com

Size isn't the only thing that matters.

Our other Big-Est retailer, Amazon.com, once billed itself as "World's Biggest Bookstore." Today, of course, we know that Amazon wants to sell everything—including kitchen sinks. The verdict is still out on that strategy and on many other elements about Amazon. (For instance, we think the company will come to regret not opening some bricks-and-mortar stores.) But regardless of where Amazon is five years from now, the company has a lot to teach about winning at Big-Est and winning at retail in general.

One thing Amazon founder and CEO Jeff Bezos preached in the early days, according to Robert Spector's book, *Amazon.com: Get Big Fast,* was that even people who loved spending time in bookstores would shop at Amazon. Why? Because Amazon offered something that could never be duplicated in a physical retail setting—the ability to buy books from the world's largest database of books. Unlike so many failed e-commerce followers, Bezos actually picked a category where the Big-Est selection proposition was achievable. Book retailing has long employed large intermediaries to warehouse assortments of books. Amazon didn't need to actually own every title it offered; it just needed the ability to quickly obtain a book and ship it. The fact that books are known commodities that can easily be shipped and are infrequently returned completed the ingredients for early success.

Few people outside the publishing industry know that there is a monstrous reference book called *Books in Print* that offers a pretty good portion of this database. But how useful or compelling for customers is a typewritten list of, say, 3 million books? Not very, so consumers were forced to rely on retailers to choose which books they would provide. Typical mall bookstores carried around 15,000 titles. Sounds impressive, but they really focused on current best-sellers and little more. Superstores like Borders and Barnes & Noble changed all of that with stores that could carry more than 150,000 titles, 10 times a mall assortment. This was wonderful for customers, but still really just a fraction of the potential assortment.

The early genius of Amazon was that it cracked the inherent problem of Internet retailing by realizing that merely being Big-Est was not the answer. What made Amazon take off, we believe, was the sophistication and great functionality of its web site. First and foremost, Amazon built a great search engine. That made its huge database of books dynamic and useful for customers. When customers searched Amazon, they found what they were looking for very easily. This was the key for Amazon, because if customers had been disappointed with searching and unable to find the books they wanted, the advantage of assortment would have been wasted, no matter how much clever marketing the company concocted.

## Big-Est: Winning with Dominant Assortments

Further, Amazon has made its web site rich with information. It features customer book reviews and notes from authors, and Amazon even suggests comparable books. An extraordinary virtual community enables Amazon to provide spectacular information about the products it sells. Today, Amazon offers song samples for CDs, so customers can listen to some snippets of the music through their computers, and it provides sample book chapters as well.

Finally, Amazon employs a relatively new trend in retail known as *mass customization,* or *one-to-one retail.* This is where Amazon is able to greet returning customers by name and show them a unique web page that features books and other products that are in line with the customer's previous purchasing patterns. The more a customer uses Amazon, the better able it is to customize an offering. Essentially, it's a way for twenty-first century retailers to tell individual customers: "We know you. We'll be your buying agent. We know what you like—and we have it."

Amazon is clearly the Big-Est book retailer today, attracting customers due to its massive selection, yet the retailer has also distinguished itself with tactics employed by small-bookstore proprietors. Amazon knows its customers by name; it knows what kinds of books they like; and it helps customers find things quickly. Those things go a long way toward making shopping easy and enjoyable.

Competition inevitably came along that could match Amazon's assortments, and many have tried, with some success, to undercut its prices. Yet Amazon has emerged as the dominant online merchant. Largest assortments, matched with placing the customer in complete control of the process, have created a lethal one-two punch. This should allow Amazon to emerge as a dominant retailer in the future, even as it grapples with the limitations of electronic commerce.

We were struck by the recent results of a consumer poll ranking customer service, as extracted from Amazon's annual report: "In this year's America's Customer Satisfaction Index, the most authoritative study of customer satisfaction, Amazon.com scored an 88, the highest score ever recorded—not just on-line, not just in retail—but the highest score ever recorded in any service industry." Amazing.

We still believe that big-Est retailers will have their place on our Est charts. However, they will need to augment the promise of having the most assortments with other compelling retail elements as well.

## TOYS "R" US

Toys "R" Us, which is currently struggling to remake itself, was America's first category killer. It took a product category—toys—that had previously been available only seasonally, and offered it year-round. Further, it presented the products in a larger-than-life setting—something most consumers had never seen before. The store's famous jingle, "I want to be a Toys "R" Us kid," said it all: "It's the biggest toy store there is, gee whiz!"

Toys "R" Us was so successful that it provided other retailers with a blueprint for the pursuit of being Big-Est. We had the company in our Est model for years, the prototypical category killer, but eventually Toys "R" Us fell out of Est for two key reasons: Toys "R" Us became complacent about taking care of customers, and it failed to keep up with competitors. The lessons of Toys "R" Us apply to all retailers: No one stays on top by default.

## Big-Est: Winning with Dominant Assortments

Toys "R" Us could have hardly been more successful, literally wiping out direct competitors (anybody remember Lionel's Kiddie City?) and becoming so powerful that it could dictate terms to vendors. Toys "R" Us became the gauge of new product success or failure. The company took its show on the road, one of the first U.S. companies to successfully expand overseas. For good measure, the company brand extended into apparel, with Kids "R" Us and Babies "R" Us. What went wrong?

Toys "R" Us began to neglect consumers, mistakenly believing that its customers had little choice about where they could buy their toys. The stores became extremely difficult to shop; their cumbersome layouts forced shoppers to walk through all of their aisles (remember Myth 1 of customer service?).

To fight shoplifting, customers could exit only through certain doors. The company cluttered its entranceways with cheap, high-margin toys in the hope that parents would cave in to demanding children. Toys "R" Us also failed to devote enough personnel to keep its stores clean and neat. The register systems were archaic and overloaded—with never enough staff to keep up with peak demand. These strategies benefited the retailer in the short term and probably made a lot of money for the company, but they did nothing for its customers. Parents came to think of a trip to Toys "R" Us about as fondly as they do about taking their kids to the dentist.

Meanwhile, competition was mounting. Specialty chains like Zany Brainy and Noodle Kidoodle were chipping away at the higher-margin educational toys business, creating a more welcoming, parent-friendly environment. They were able to launch more education-oriented toys and create a reasonably sized alternative outlet for merchandise. Focusing

77

on toys that had an educational component endeared them to the parents and grandparents of the world.

Wal-Mart, Kmart, and Target began to increase their toy assortments. Families were already shopping at these stores on a regular basis. Buying toys at a discount store saved time and money, and the category was a big winner for the discounters. Because of their broader merchandise mix, these discounters could undercut Toys "R" Us on key items. These chains now offer very credible assortments of toys from the key manufacturers, and they come close to Toys "R" Us in assortments in many cases. In 1998, Wal-Mart surpassed Toys "R" Us as the nation's "biggest toy store there is," claiming 17.4 percent of the roughly $20 billion industry, compared with 16.8 percent for Toys "R" Us, according to the research firm NPD Group. Toys "R" Us's market share had fallen to 16.5 percent in 2000, down from a 25 percent market share in the mid-1990s.

Finally, the nature of toys changed, and Toys "R" Us failed to change fast enough to keep up. The line between electronics and toys has increasingly blurred, with computers and video games vying for the attention of younger and younger children. Toys "R" Us was late to the game in these categories, and retailers like Best Buy were the early beneficiaries.

Under new leadership, Toys "R" Us substantially revamped all of its stores, making them more customer-friendly and broadening assortments to vie with the expanded competition. Its flagship store in Manhattan is spectacular and includes a 100-foot indoor Ferris wheel. They have closed down Kids "R" Us, yet another entrant into the Retail Black Hole. The company is now taking the appropriate steps to win back customers; hopefully, it is not too late. Our Est chart would have told Toys "R" Us to get started many years earlier, even when it was still on top.

## Big-Est: Winning with Dominant Assortments

One of the concepts we frequently mention is the *retail inflection point*—the point in a retailer's life cycle where a significant change occurs that strategically impacts the company's future direction. Think of it as the point at which a retailer's future turns positive or negative. It is not always obvious to read, and companies often respond too late to external factors, which was certainly the case at Toys "R" Us.

## INCREDIBLE UNIVERSE

Incredible? Yes. Profitable? No.

A now-defunct home electronics chain called Incredible Universe epitomizes the lesson that you don't win at Big-Est by having the most products. It also serves as an example of what can happen when a retailer tries to be "All-Est."

We know this story well because we were hired to lead the concept development team for Incredible Universe, which was part of Tandy Corp. (now RadioShack Corp.). Incredible Universe was born in the early 1990s, at a time when Tandy's RadioShack stores were struggling and the company, in turn, was expanding into sexier new concepts. The company had already had some early success at this with its Computer City stores, a computer store category killer.

With Incredible Universe, Tandy was essentially looking to create the Consumer Electronics Show for consumers, the incredible general trade show that showcases the latest and greatest products in a glitzy setting. Incredible Universe set out to outdo the assortments of Circuit City and Best Buy. If those stores carried 250 TV sets, Incredible Universe would carry 700. While outdoing the competition was a potentially worthy goal, Incredible Universe took it to an absurd extreme. Let's say a customer wanted a TV with picture-in-picture and stereo surround sound. A good merchant might offer two to three different models with these features, at varying price points, with slightly different corollary features. Incredible Universe would offer 12 TVs with picture-in-picture and stereo surround that were virtually the same. That forces the customer to do unnecessary work making a mostly meaningless decision—work the merchant should have done for the customer.

Circuit City and Best Buy stores at that time were about 25,000 square feet. Incredible Universe stores were more than 100,000 square feet—that's five times larger than the competition. That extra assortment took more room to display and warehouse. Incredible Universe's Big-Est strategy also meant it had to have massive stores and large inventories. As a result, the stores were too expensive to operate. It also meant that slow-turning inventory (merchandise that doesn't sell often) became a huge problem.

Incredible Universe also suffered because, in addition to Big-Est, it wanted to be everything for customers, from Cheap-Est to Hot-Est to Easy-Est. Tandy made big investments in these stores, and it had some success in producing tremendous store volumes at select stores. Employees were well trained and helpful. They had slick radio equipment that ensured large products were ready for pickup when customers pulled their cars around to retrieve large items like big-screen TVs. Not surprisingly, many customers loved Incredible Universe.

In hindsight, we contend that Tandy's management was right about a lot of things. When Incredible Universe was launched, Best Buy and Circuit City stores were about 20,000 square feet. Today, those stores range in size from 30,000 to 50,000 square feet. Customers indeed wanted more selection and authority. Incredible Universe also expanded the boundaries of a home electronics store by selling both hardware (e.g., stereos) and software (e.g., CDs) and by selling small electric appliances like blenders and toasters in addition to major appliances. In both instances, the company was ahead of its time, as these features are now standard at its competitors.

Incredible Universe stores were also among the first to have play areas for children and small restaurants for adults to eat—typically either McDonald's or Pizza Hut. The chain innovated in lots of ways that hit the right buttons with customers.

But as part of the planning, a painful miscalculation was made relative to product mix. It was assumed that home computers would make up about 15 percent of the business. Instead, computers ended up being closer to 35 percent of sales, and due to extremely competitive pressures the margins were much lower than planned. While the stores did attain the sales volume Tandy was anticipating, gross margins were far lower than expected. Another missed assumption had to do with advertising. Originally, it was assumed the massive, prominently located stores would work as billboards (similar to Ikea), which would mean that Incredible Universe could get away with little or no advertising. The company soon found out that in this highly promotional category—where competitors fatten newspapers with weekly ads—Incredible Universe needed to spend as much on advertising as its competitors.

Incredible Universe was an example of trying to be too many Ests at once, and because of the high costs and huge resource requirements, Tandy eventually shut down the unprofitable venture. Even though it achieved an Est position, it wasn't economically sustainable. We have often said that the intersection of all Est points is the Black Hole. Incredible Universe was a living example of the theory.

At McMillan|Doolittle we have helped launch dozens of retail concepts over the years, and we know there's never one simple explanation of success or failure. Typically, though, successful new retail concepts meet consumer demand, leverage a retailer's internal capabilities, carve out a defensible market niche, and can be operated profitably.

The bottom line for Incredible Universe was that the stores didn't make any money. Misinterpreting Big-Est played a large role in the chain's demise, as it strained the economics while not providing a meaningful enough difference to customers.

CHAPTER FIVE

# HOT-EST: WINNING WITH FASHION

Stores that win on fashion are Hot-Est. When we talk about Hot-Est, we're not talking about the latest styles to strut off the runways in Paris or Milan. Far from it. We define Hot-Est retailers as stores that have the latest products just as customers begin to buy them in volume. We're talking about mass fashion, not couture getups that look pretty (although they often look pretty unusual) and sell to only a tiny fraction of the public who can afford such luxuries. Fashion can be a remarkable driver of sales growth in all channels—Hot-Est is indeed an Est that transcends product boundaries. (See Figure 5.1.)

There's an element of fashion in every facet of retail, from grocery stores to hardware stores. Want proof? One of the hottest retailers in the country today is Krispy Kreme, which is selling a decidedly traditional product, the doughnut. Yet we think Krispy Kreme is really selling (in addition to a decadent product that tastes pretty good) *fashion*. The company has managed to package the donut into a retail experience, with hot products coming off the visible production lines and customer lines snaking out the door. The combination of nostalgia, a great-tasting product, and marvelous PR

**FIGURE 5.1**   Est Chart: Hot-Est Retailers

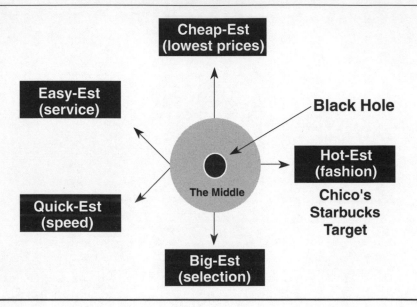

has made the old-fashioned, bad-for-you, anti–health-trend dough-nut one of the hottest fashion items in recent years. One of our recent surreal experiences was attending the opening of a Krispy Kreme in Harrod's flagship London store, a retail fashion institution. The Krispy Kreme "Hot Donuts" sign now shares space with one of retail's most elegant stores. We sipped champagne in Harrod's grand ballroom while munching on hot doughnuts. Go figure.

We have been preaching the power of fashion in industries unaccustomed to hearing the word. We worked with the Vons gro-cery stores (now part of Safeway) to build one of the first fashion-driven supermarkets, Pavilions, which remains an unqualified success today. Pavilions was one of the first stores of its kind to feature sushi bars, in-store bakeries, prepared foods, housewares, specialty and gourmet foods, and a host of other products we routinely take for granted in today's modern stores.

In many categories, being Hot-Est can be a nice complement to an existing business, a key differentiator from a competitor. Stores can build reputations around consistently having the latest products, brands, colors, or styles that set them apart from competitors. We have seen fashion at work in the most mundane of places, from auto parts stores to lumberyards.

In other categories of retail, most notably apparel, fashion is often the main differentiator. A large number of brands vie for the label of Hot-Est, carrying the right style and fashion with the right target customer. It is a tough proposition to continually be on the right side of the fashion spectrum, but the rewards are vast. Margins in the Hot-Est business can be spectacular, as the consumer is thinking about something other than price.

Being Hot-Est is one of the more unusual Ests because it is not built on the same rational decision points that drive price, assortment, or location. We freely admit that the ability to be hottest contains a bit of magic as well—a certain undefinable characteristic that sets one retailer apart from another. The overused word today is *branding:* This word connotes the ability to distinguish between a product or service on differentiators that have their own unique power. Coca-Cola, one of the world's greatest brands, is selling flavored, carbonated water, but the brand stands for so much more than that, keying in on lifestyle, nostalgia, and other emotional characteristics that on the surface seem completely absurd for a commodity product.

The same holds true in the retail world as well: World-class Est retailers have a powerful emotional element that drives the business along with purely rational characteristics.

Perhaps the most problematic challenge thrown at the Est theory over the years is the lack of ability to account for the magic of a brand. Shouldn't there be an Est for, say, highest quality? Our response, typically, has been to fall back on the Est model. Tiffany, for example, is a stunningly successful jewelry retailer. The brand conveys almost mythical style and elegance. Isn't Tiffany selling the best-quality jewelry in the world? Perhaps. We believe they are also selling the key element of Hot-Est: the right product as it comes into fashion. In the case of Tiffany, this means unique design sold with wonderful elegance and flourish. If the product itself isn't Hot-Est (and a great deal of what Tiffany sells isn't terribly unique), the brand conveys a sense of Hot-Est. The famed Tiffany blue box speaks volumes about what Hot-Est is all about: The buyer feels that he or she has come to the right place and has received something special. You can call it wonderful branding, and it is. It is also a demonstration of Hot-Est.

On a mass scale, think of retail stores as trend conductors. Hot-Est retailers should be experts in the products they carry and have a passion for sharing that expertise and for selling customers the latest, most fashionable products. Fashion is the great energizer of sales in retailing, one of the key reasons customers come back on a regular basis to trendsetting retailers. We think of fashion as having the right stuff—and having it in stock while it's hot.

The upsides of being Hot-Est are tremendous volume and a lot of traffic in your store. The downside, equally significant, is the risk of stores loaded with trend-wrong merchandise on the clearance shelves. Being a fashion merchant is inherently risky, and it also means that business is bound to be cyclical—sometimes hot, sometimes cold. Hot-Est is very difficult to maintain year after year. That's why our list of Hot-Est retailers changes frequently. It's also a difficult proposition to communicate to customers. Simply saying, "We're hot!" doesn't cut it. That's not true for Cheap-Est retailers, on the other hand, who do have the luxury to be straightforward with marketing, à la Wal-Mart's "Always Low Prices."

Of course, most stores want to be trend-right. But Hot-Est retailers have established that as their core mission. They build their businesses around organizational structures and distribution systems that allow them to spot trends quickly and then get the right merchandise on their sales floors just as the trend accelerates. Hot-Est retailers also have the ability to recover quickly when they miss, which is what one of our original Hot-Est retailers, The Gap, has had a difficult time doing in recent years.

Being Hot-Est requires superior merchants to make good bets consistently. That necessitates staying very close to customers—because you won't survive by simply guessing what customers will want in the future. Fashion retailers must correctly predict what customers will want in the future to win at being Hot-Est. That requires watching and studying leading-edge indicators, the places where trends are born—whether fashion houses in Milan and Paris, food purveyors in Seattle, or teenagers on the streets of Harlem and the beaches of Los Angeles.

Once you've spotted the trend and interpreted it to mesh with your customers and your store's identity, then you must get the product to market quickly. That requires a supply chain that's built for speed, as well as a knack for timing, which is a key element for fashion merchants. Hot-Est retailers know when to get in to products, then amass big inventories as demand peaks, and exit at the right time. Hot-Est retailers are rarely caught with yesterday's styles. They are sophisticated about their promotional strategies, and regularly change the look and layout of their stores to keep things fresh for shoppers. Some of the newest and most innovative fashion merchants, such as Zara, H&M, and Hot Topic, are drastically altering the game with their incredible speed to market.

Other Hot-Est retailers today include Chico's, which sells loosely structured women's apparel to baby boomers. Their hottest secret? Being right for a group of consumers (aging baby boomers) who are often ignored by the trendier brands targeting the elusive size 6. Chico's sells outfits that are flattering for their demographic and has also democratized sizes, opting for a simple 1, 2, 3 sizing scheme. Whole Foods has elevated fashion to a high art form in the food business. Sure, the company is selling natural food products that are better for you, and it is devoted to this cause, but we would also argue that Whole Foods has taken this good-for-you mission and wrapped it around a wonderful, expensive supermarket. Rather than customers complaining about the high prices, they justify the added expense by knowing they are taking better care of themselves and their families. Hot Topic sells apparel to teenagers, a notoriously fickle consumer group. It seems that few companies stay hot with this consumer for very long. Hot Topic's secret? It's a fast follower. Its buyers studiously monitor pop culture and are blindingly fast in offering the styles that the latest popular lead singer on an MTV video is wearing. Hot Topic doesn't set any trends, but is simply a fast follower—and is equally fast dumping the stuff that isn't working. The company keeps its stores small and manageable and hasn't overextended. This has enabled Hot Topic to stay hot to a tough customer demographic for a long time. Starbucks is another excellent example, opening stores at a rate of more than 1,000 per year. The best statistic about the Starbucks phenomenon? Despite its incredible growth, coffee consumption in the United States is declining and has been since Starbucks' inception. The genius of this chain was turning a 25-cent cup of coffee into a $4 life experience.

On a mass scale, we think the most powerful example, one that's managed to stay Hot-Est for a long time, is the discount chain Target.

## Hot-Est: Target

It's futile to make the case that any retailer other than Wal-Mart is the most amazing success story in the history of American retailing. We wouldn't argue, and neither would Target vice chairman Gerald Storch, who was quoted in the April 2, 2001, issue of *DSN Retailing Today* as saying, "Wal-Mart is the greatest retailer that ever was, and we have to compete with them on a regular basis. There is no one else that has been able to compete with Wal-Mart and thrive. Very few have been able to compete with them and survive." Storch also inferred that Target itself is an amazing success story, and we agree. Target may be the best example of the power and potential of Est retailing. (See Table 5.1.)

Target, which was originally part of Dayton Hudson Corp., took a unique approach when it set out to establish a discount store. In addition to battling it out at discount prices, Target also decided to go after a very attractive consumer segment. Leveraging its core competencies as a department store merchant that operated the leading chains in Minneapolis (Dayton's) and Detroit (Hudson's), Target focused on attracting women with children who live in the suburbs. It engineered a more pleasant shopping experience than its discount store rivals and developed a simple design and logo scheme to support it, but the main driver of success was focused on fashion appeal. Target succeeded in offering competitive prices and improving the shopping experiences over those of Wal-Mart and Kmart, but the chain's amazing performance was rooted in its success at being Hot-Est.

In hindsight, it seems obvious. The company's department store legacy gave it a knack for fashion and access to

**TABLE 5.1**  Performance of Hot-Est Retailer: Target

|  | 1993 | 2002 | Compound Annual Growth Rate (%), 1993–2002 |
| --- | --- | --- | --- |
| Net sales ($ millions) | $11,743 | $36,917 | 13.5 |
| Net income* ($ millions) | $375 | $1,654 | 18 |
| Operating profit (%) | 5.6 | 9.4 | N/A |
| Number of stores | 554 | 1,147 | 8.4 |

*Reflects amount for total company, including Target, Marshall Field's, Mervyns, and so on.

better brands that couldn't be matched by Wal-Mart founder Sam Walton or the Kresges, who gave us Kmart and who had operated a chain of five-and-dime stores. At the time, the oxymoronic concept of "upscale discount" was not only unproven, it was completely unknown. Today, it is a niche that Target has to itself.

Our cofounder, Norm McMillan, was part of the Dayton Hudson team charged with creating the vision for Target stores in the 1970s. The group produced an elegantly simple paper brochure (it's carefully stored in one of our filing cabinets) that says almost exactly the same thing about Target as does Target Corp.'s glossy, 44-page 2000 annual report. The annual report reads: "Target Corp. is committed to delivering fashion newness and distinction, compelling value and overall shopping excitement. . . . At Target, the strength of our brand reflects our keen focus on offering quality, trend-right merchandise at great prices, through powerful presentations in attractive stores."

Norm's team said, in essence, the very same thing nearly 25 years earlier (with greater economy of language): "Target is a trend merchant. Target sells higher quality merchandise." We mention this not just to boast about our cofounder. We mention it to illustrate how a retailer's Est position can be so well articulated that it becomes a timeless compass to guide the enterprise.

Naturally, staying on course is the trick. One thing Target did to guard itself against the fickle nature of Hot-Est was to create a large and fairly autonomous 23-person "trend team." The demise of many Hot-Est retailers is often linked to losing key personnel, usually merchants, who, being creative talents, are known to be temperamental. Target's trend team worked to combat that by indoctrinating a large number of people into the practice of trend spotting, thereby making the company less vulnerable to losing one or two merchant superstars. The team's existence and vaunted status also institutionalized the notion that Target's core business would be fashion. As mentioned earlier, Target had a head start because it was able to leverage supplier contacts from its department stores. Target executives knew what was fashionable, and equally important, they knew who could deliver knockoff versions that Target could sell markedly cheaper than the originals.

Target has learned not only where to find knockoff merchandise, but also has become adept at having the merchandise made and shipped halfway around the world in a hurry. That's a key component of Hot-Est, because you have to have the trend-right merchandise just as demand is peaking. Production or distribution delays make that impossible.

Target also has distinguished itself with its marketing. It was the first, and to our knowledge remains the only, discount store to host a fashion show in New York City. It runs ads in fashion magazines. Its TV and magazine commercials are all a little edgy, which can be puzzling for older, less affluent consumers. The ads burnish an image of Target as young, fun, and hip. The ads don't mention price or try to pitch Target as a discount store. The ads, known for incorporating consumer products in unconventional ways, are clever and subtle because they speak to customers who can afford to shop at department stores but also value a good deal.

We'd be remiss if we didn't mention that Target's store layout and execution also ring true to its status as an upscale discounter. Since Target's core customers are more affluent than those of Wal-Mart, they have higher expectations of a shopping experience. That's why Target doesn't stack merchandise atop pallets or allow vendors to set up chintzy cardboard displays in its stores. Target sought to make shopping in its stores palatable—even exciting—for people who can afford to shop anywhere. In this regard, actress Sarah Jessica Parker did some free publicity several years ago for Target when she appeared on NBC's Conan O'Brien show. Apparently Parker, a trendsetting New York actress even before the blockbuster success of HBO's *Sex in the City,* had visited a Target store for the first time just before her late-night TV appearance. Somehow, the subject came up, and Parker proceeded to spend most of the interview raving about Target. There were so many products, she gushed, so cheap, and there was so much cute merchandise. O'Brien joked about how the interview had turned into a Target commercial. Better, it had turned into buzz—the kind of buzz that makes Hot-Est retailers.

The other key element of this control over its stores, and the one that is really fueling Target's growth today, is the chain's inherent understanding of the power of branding. While Norm's team never used this word in the original document, they sure understood its power. Whereas so many other stores are content to allow their vendors to clutter their aisles with endless displays of merchandise (sold at attractive prices with ample incentive for the retailer to carry them), Target understands the danger of this trap: If all retailers carry the same stuff and use the same displays from the same vendors, price automatically becomes the key differentiator. A customer simply can't tell one store from another. One of our colleagues derisively calls this "surrender to the vendor." Target does no such thing.

Another great source of buzz in recent years that has fueled Target's Hot-Est positioning has been the development of Target-exclusive products from celebrity designers. It began in 1999 with architect Michael Graves. Graves had designed products in the past for the upscale Italian accessories-maker

Alessi—things like $120 teapots. When Graves agreed to design products for a discount chain, fashionistas took note. As *Time* magazine stated in its March 2000 cover story about a nationwide trend of the masses craving high-style design: "[Target] has become the talk of Madison Avenue, not to mention Main Street." In a similar vein, *Newsweek* devoted an ample portion of its October 2003 design issue to the advancements in fashion being made at Target.

Now Target is looking to build on the success it's had with Michael Graves by bringing in other designers, including apparel designer Mossimo Gianulli and makeup artist Sonia Kashuk. Additionally, Target has brought in some well-known brands that have upscale cachet, like Calphalon cookwear, Woolrich and Waverly linens, Eddie Bauer camping gear, and Virgin electronics. While the chain has had some misses of late, notably a Phillipe Starck line that failed to catch on with consumers, it is quick to move when it doesn't meet success, a vital characteristic of a fashion retailer. While Starck's fashions did not catch on at Target, the flamboyant designer Isaac Mizrahi recently launched a comprehensive line. Target is fast becoming the place for designers to launch wonderful products at affordable prices—in essence taking fashion to the masses. Designer Liz Lange has developed a wonderful maternity line, and Todd Oldham has fashioned funky styles that are geared for the dorm room. The hits seem to keep on coming. This Hot-Est retailer is on a roll.

Target hardly seems through in carrying out its mission of hottest. Like Wal-Mart, food has become Target's major expansion thrust. Not surprisingly, Target has done a first-rate job of transferring its concept of upscale discount store to its fledgling grocery business. SuperTarget stores, which combine its full discount store offerings and a full-service supermarket, include artisan breads, top-grade meats and produce, and premium brands like Starbucks coffee, Krispy Kreme doughnuts, and Eli's Cheesecakes. While Target's supercenter concept is well done, it remains to be seen whether Target can succeed with groceries and whether customers will be drawn to Target's fashion-food proposition.

Groceries have been a great success for Wal-Mart, but it's probably more likely that discount store shoppers would prefer Cheap-Est groceries to Hot-Est groceries. Of course, people once wondered whether "cheap and chic" was a viable strategy.

The clear danger for Target, which seems to be walking a precariously fine line, is that distinction between following fashion and attempting to set it. Target does a dazzling job of breaking through the norms in its marketing and merchandising approach. The one concern (and a Hot-Est danger) is in becoming *too* hip. Target can get ahead of its customers, who aren't nearly as sophisticated as the slick merchants and advertisers who are peddling advice. A trip through a Target store still reveals Middle America at its best: aspirational, to be sure, but this is still a mom with kids and a budget who is not necessarily glued to the headlines from Milan. Fashions by Michael Graves worked because they were both stylish and practical; Phillipe Starck's didn't follow the same formula. We worry when a retailer loses sight of its fundamental mission (and target customer). Target has it all working right now, but no Est lasts forever.

## THE GAP

The Gap is one of America's great Hot-Est retailers. It has been adorning (almost a fixture on) our Est charts for as long as we have been using the model. In a way, Gap is the quintessential Hot-Est retailer, selling apparel to the masses and winning time and time again. Still, as with every Hot-Est retailer, staying on the charts is enormously difficult. Gap, however, has had more staying power than anyone. That's why it was particularly shocking when in the middle of 2000, Gap's performance started to markedly deteriorate. In fact, the company that could do no wrong was now considered a dinosaur. America's most profitable retailer suddenly became a potential candidate for the Black Hole. While Gap still sells acres of khaki pants and denim shirts, it lately lost its way as a Hot-Est retailer. The Gap, now firmly in turnaround mode, offers a powerful cautionary tale.

Gap epitomized mass fashion in the mid- to late-1990s. Time and again it hit (some say created) *the* trend of the season, stocked its stores chock-full of the stuff, and watched its sales explode. This formula led to mind-numbing profits and return on investment for its shareholders. Gap was consistently a fantastic Wall Street performer as well as a retail star.

Gap also managed to hang onto its evolving customer base by developing distinctly positioned stores—Banana Republic and Old Navy, the fastest-growing new retail chain ever. Banana Republic catered to Gap customers when they grew up and were looking for more sophisticated styles. Old Navy catered to younger Gap customers and budget-conscious families by carrying simple, inexpensive knockoffs of Gap fashion.

When it was winning, Gap's stores reflected the latest trends, with updates of Gap basics like khakis and ribbed T-shirts.

Its stores were crisp and clean and conveyed a consistent fashion sense. Gap was quickly opening new stores, and it was building larger stores to bolster its sales gains.

The downside of all this growth was that Gap became ubiquitous, and things that are ubiquitous are not hot. You'll recall our definition of Hot-Est: "having the latest products just as customers begin to buy them in volume." Gap kept going with what worked, pronouncing denim or colors as *the* trend, but in doing that, Gap was pushing apparel that everyone "already had bought in volume." In other words, Gap was pushing clothes that weren't fashionable. America already had a closet loaded with those Gap fashions—it didn't need anymore.

On the other extreme, Gap also found itself being outdone by competitors like Abercrombie & Fitch, Wet Seal, and American Eagle. These stores were doing a better job of being hotter and cooler for teens. While Gap's demographic was aging, these retailers took a decidedly narrower focus. (Teens were seeing their parents buying things for themselves at Gap—who wants to shop where Mom shops?) Essentially, Gap had become the general store that was losing customers to specialists who picked away at targeted customer segments.

To counter these problems, Gap tried its hand at some eclectic, high-fashion clothes like orchid-colored leather jackets and crocheted halter tops. But customers didn't go for the edgier fashions with muddier colors, and Gap was derided for its fashion gaffes. The core problem with Gap's strategy was that customers never expected (or wanted) Gap to be a fashion leader. Gap is about mass fashion, not high fashion. More damaging, Gap wasn't following its own direction—it found itself in the uncharacteristic place of following others.

Of course, Gap has missed on fashion before—that simply comes with the territory of trying to be Hot-Est. But when it was a nimbler company with fewer and smaller stores it recovered quickly. That was a big part of Gap's success—it could come back quickly, because if it missed the fashion trend, it would sell through the merchandise in a matter of weeks and catch the next trend. Gap was famous for turning over inventory every six weeks and making quick corrections on the fly.

What was unique about its problems from 2000 to 2003 was that this was a very prolonged dip. (April of 2002 marked 24 consecutive months of declining "same-store sales," which measures sales against the same month a year earlier, excluding those stores open less than a year.) This dip is not just about erring on the season's fashions. This time Gap is facing more competition with too many stores and too much space. Gap opened lots of stores and got a lot bigger in a hurry, doubling its square footage from 1997 to 2000. Filling those large stores makes Gap less distinctive and less nimble.

Shocking things were happening at a corporate level as well. The legendary Mickey Drexler left Gap. More than anyone, he was synonymous with The Gap's success, single-handedly setting the fashion course at all of the company's divisions. It seemed improbable that he could be replaced.

Yet in our November 2002 *Retail Watch*, we declared that The Gap was back. Gone were the wild fashions that didn't catch on. Back was the classic formula of basics with a twist. Gap is back in fashion, nursing the edges but not taking as many risks. We have noted the steady improvement in sales as a good indicator that the company is back on track. It seems to have fixed fashion (for now). It may take longer to solve the issue of ubiquity and real estate.

We are convinced, more than ever, of the power of Hot-Est. It can nurture and burn. Gap is living proof.

**CHAPTER SIX**

# EASY-EST: WINNING WITH SOLUTION-ORIENTED SERVICE

Developing a position that explains how retailers win by providing superior customer service was probably the most difficult part of creating the Est theory. We admit, the issue was partly semantics. "Customer Service–Est" just doesn't cut it. In addition to sounding awkward, Customer Service–Est doesn't adequately address the key issues for retailers. We really don't believe that retailers win by providing outstanding customer service. It can be critically important, but it doesn't explain the whole picture.

We were also mindful that many retailers don't understand what customer service is really all about, as outlined in significant detail in our earlier discussion on customer service. Retailers basically have a different definition of customer service than do customers. We think it's best to stick with the customers' definition (which we developed after years of observing consumer behavior and analyzing consumer research). The customer's definition of service is: (1) knowing what I want and having it in stock; (2) helping me find the product I'm looking for easily without wasting my time; (3) providing information to answer my questions and assist me in making an intelligent choice—with signs, brochures, a salesperson, or via the Internet; and after you've done the first three right; (4) having friendly, knowl-edgeable people.

After reviewing this definition and studying retailers that win because of their exemplary customer service, a clearer theme emerged—*ease of use* for customers.

- Customers want an experience that makes shopping easy and hassle-free.
- They want an experience that makes it easy for them to solve whatever problem they have, from something as mundane as buying gas to something as complex as actually purchasing a car.
- They want an experience that enables them to easily choose the available option that is right for them.
- They want a solution proposed by retailers who know their stuff and who understand customers' needs, wants, and aspirations.

That's how we came up with Easy-Est.

Originally, Easy-Est included retailers such as Nordstrom and Saturn along with Walgreens and McDonald's. An odd list for sure, and it led to some vocal dissent among those who heard the theory. Years later, we added Quick-Est to differentiate between speed-oriented service and solution-oriented service. A smart move, even if it messed with the neat symmetry of our Est model.

How do we define an Easy-Est retailer? Simply put, these are retailers who help customers solve problems. They often cater to customers who do not know exactly what they want. When these customers set out to shop, they're looking for ideas as well as products or services that will help them find a good solution. Customers also want the comfort of knowing that they bought their product from the right place. (See Figure 6.1.)

**FIGURE 6.1**   Est Chart: Easy-Est Retailers

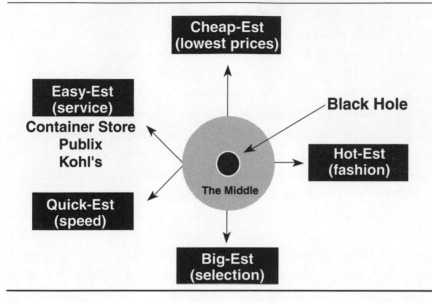

In turn, Easy-Est retailers can do much more than simply solve a problem. They help create ideas, provide assurance, offer an enriching experience, and provide information to help customers understand their options and make decisions easily.

Attempting to win being Easy-Est may be the most difficult Est position to execute. The others are rooted, essentially, in a single merchandise-related proposition. Cheap-Est stores have the lowest-priced merchandise. Hot-Est stores have the latest merchandise. Big-Est stores have the best selection of merchandise.

Easy-Est is a more complex, more experiential proposition that combines product, service, and price. Easy-Est retailers must consider everything about a customer's shopping trip and then try to deliver a solution that creates an ideal experience. Easy-Est retailers must be masters, in short, of almost all the key retail disciplines in order to be successful.

Nordstrom is a great example of an Easy-Est retailer. The Seattle-based chain was renowned for its well-trained salespeople who knock themselves out to satisfy customers. But that's not the only facet of what made Nordstrom Easy-Est. Nordstrom was successful at Easy-Est because its stores were engineered from a customer's perspective. For example, at Nordstrom, a salesperson can assemble an entire outfit for a customer rather than being forced to pass the customer off to another salesperson in a different department of the store. That practice comes from viewing things from the customer's vantage point rather than the territorial concerns of the retailer.

What made Saturn an Easy-Est retailer was that it eliminated customers' least favorite parts of buying a car—the haggling, the secretive prices, and the high-pressure sales tactics. Saturn succeeded in providing customers the assurance that they were buying a car at the right place and that they were being told information they needed. Many elements of the Saturn process are now being replicated at places like CarMax, a later entry into the Easy-Est category.

Consider how Pottery Barn and Crate & Barrel provide Easy-Est solutions (where furniture warehouses do not). Say you're looking for a new floor lamp for your living room. Both Pottery Barn and Crate & Barrel sell several different styles of floor lamps, but their stores don't feature a lighting department. Instead, they display floor lamps along with other living room furniture (sofas, end tables, TV cabinets), which ultimately suggests, "Here's how to make your living room look beautiful." Pottery Barn and Crate & Barrel stores are selling customers the complete solution, not just a product.

Furniture warehouses, on the other hand, have dozens of floor lamps merchandised together in a lighting department. There's probably a larger selection, but with its category-merchandising approach—versus Pottery Barn and Crate & Barrel's lifestyle or solution-based merchandising approach—the warehouse stores don't give customers any idea how the floor lamps can beautify a room. That's why stores like Pottery Barn and Crate & Barrel are

# Easy-Est: Winning with Solution-Oriented Service

Easy-Est. They provide ideas and solutions for people looking to beautify their homes. Item/category merchants, like furniture warehouses, are commodity stores. Customers think of them as places to buy sofas, tables, and lamps. Period.

More central to the experience is having the right merchandise for a particular customer segment. Warehouse furniture stores probably carry an assortment of floor lamps that includes many styles and prices. That makes sense, of course, in trying to serve a large, disparate clientele. But it's not really a benefit to the individual customer, who invariably prefers a certain style and also has a certain price range he or she is willing to pay. Customers don't want to see every lamp ever made, just the ones that fit into their lifestyle.

Pottery Barn and Crate, on the other hand, try to serve customers by taking what is now called a lifestyle merchandising approach: They offer just a few styles that they believe appeal to their narrow band of customers. For these customers, stores like Pottery Barn and Crate offer a much easier solution than furniture warehouses, which force customers to sift through hundreds of floor lamps to find three or four that match their taste.

The great challenge of the lifestyle approach is that Pottery Barn and Crate & Barrel must be great at merchandise selection because their assortments are limited. In turn, they must be very in step with their target customers. Being a lifestyle merchant requires the skills of Hot-Est and Easy-Est in tandem: These stores have to select the right products.

The big key for Easy-Est retailers is viewing the world from a customer's perspective. Easy-Est retailers must be locked into customer attitudes and trends. They also must organize their businesses around the customer's interest rather than their own interest. That means different things for different retailers. For Pottery Barn and Crate & Barrel, it involves investing heavily in merchandise selection and visual display. For stores like Nordstrom, it involves motivating employees to serve.

While cultivating great people is often an attribute of Easy-Est retailers, great customer service is not dependent on having wonderful salespeople. One of our favorite stories about this comes from the retail banking industry. Automated teller machines (ATMs) were probably the most significant customer service advancement in retail banking in the 1990s. Customers kept telling banks they wanted easier access to their cash. The answer wasn't more friendly tellers or expanded teller hours. The answer was a technology that eliminated tellers from the transaction—and made getting cash a lot easier for customers.

One store that's winning big today at Easy-Est is the junior department store Kohl's. Like the ATM, Kohl's doesn't do it with more people. Kohl's does it through merchandise organization, layout, and presentation in a self-help format that caters to middle-income families. Kohl's tailors (edits) an assortment of brand-name goods at low prices and keeps it in stock all the time. Its stores are located in easy-to-get-to shopping centers that allow customers to park closer to the door and eliminate the hassles of a mall. It is clear where to buy products and it is also clear where the checkouts are. In many ways, Kohl's has simplified the department store experience (a maze of departments, floors, and checkouts) in much the same way Saturn has revolutionized new car buying.

Other stores winning today at Easy-Est include Pottery Barn, Crate & Barrel, the used-auto retailer CarMax, Publix supermarkets, and the Container Store, a small chain that sells products that "help organize your life."

### Easy-Est: Container Store

The Container Store, a private company based in Dallas, is known for being so good at providing storage solutions that it often solves problems people didn't even know they had.

Only the most advanced marketers progress to the point of meeting unarticulated wants. That's the power of Container Store.

Container Store is zealous about product knowledge and its mission to educate customers. Its employees are required to do 235 hours of product training in their first year and 162 hours each year afterward. The average in the retail industry is 10 hours of product training a year, according to a *USA Today* article.

Container Store employees also take part in twice-daily store "huddles," where employees discuss sales goals and swap product information—including a tip of the day about one particular product. Associates learn from each other, and they learn from customers, who sometimes figure out new ways to use storage products. This customer/employee orientation enables Container Store to predict problems and offer creative solutions. Its employees know their stuff, and they can talk in detail about product benefits and how to innovatively solve customers' problems.

On one of our recent trips to the Container Store, we engaged a salesperson to help with a common problem of business travelers—how to organize all those patch cords, plugs, connectors, and adaptors that inevitably accompany the collection of electronic devices we now carry in our briefcases. This is the perfect type of product for Container Store. Unfortunately, the perfect organizer for these items doesn't exist. Nor is there an aisle in the store marked for business travel organization. However, employees were quick to suggest a variety of innovative ways to store these items using products that were designed for another function. Not only did we get the solution, but we had a range of choices, colors, and options. The irony of this encounter, and many like it at Container Store, was that we hadn't walked into the store with this in mind, but we did walk out with plenty of merchandise.

The Container Store also owns the distinction of having perhaps the best-merchandised and most productive check-outs in all of retail. Its stores offer a spectacular display of gadgets and doodads that tempt the customer with solutions to unmet needs. Rather than being turned off by last-minute sales, the typical response of customers is gratitude for having been offered more ways to solve their problems. This is yet another sign of a great Easy-Est retailer who combines a multitude of skill sets.

Container Store employees also adopt a service-oriented, problem-solver mentality because that's the emphasis of its culture. This gives employees an uncanny ability to help customers. They don't overwhelm shoppers with sales assistance, but they are there when needed. We've often said that the best level of customer service would come from mind readers—employees who can sense when customers need help and when they need to be left alone.

Container Store is regularly near the top of *Fortune* magazine's list of best places to work. Store employment annual turnover is 10 to 15 percent—numbers that are unheard of in today's retail world. The company pays twice as much as some other retailers, but Container Store executives reason that the company is getting a bargain because they believe one good employee is worth three average ones. In fact, Container Store breaks a tried-and-true retail maxim: Rather than striving for productivity (higher sales means that labor costs go down as a percentage of store sales), the company chooses to keep its labor at a fixed percentage of sales. The busier the Container Store, the more sales help is available. Imagine that. Most important, Container Store encourages its sales associates to contribute ideas. The end result is a sales

# Easy-Est: Winning with Solution-Oriented Service

force that's knowledgeable and highly motivated to provide solutions and help make shopping easy and enjoyable for customers.

Container Store's secrets to success, as is true of so many Est examples, are hardly secret. The company's ideas, like the merchandise its sells, are there for the taking. Yet we can think of few retailers who are ready to adopt this customer-comes-first (so-we-better-have-fantastic-employees) mentality of the Container Store. Its relatively small size perhaps suggests that this isn't an easy concept to copy. That's precisely what the Container Store believes as well, which is why it has grown slowly and successfully, without succumbing to the temptations of fast growth and fast riches.

## Easy-Est: Publix

Publix, a privately held supermarket chain based in Florida, developed the slogan "Where shopping is a pleasure" more than 60 years ago. (See Table 6.1.)

Publix founder George Jenkins used to drive a car (long before there were such things as compact cars) through grocery aisles during grand openings to show off Publix's wide

**TABLE 6.1**   Performance of Easy-Est Retailer: Publix

|  | 1993 | 2002 | CAGR (%), 1993–2002 |
|---|---|---|---|
| Net sales ($ millions) | $7,473 | $16,027 | 8.8 |
| Net income ($ millions) | $180 | $632 | 14.6 |
| Operating profit (%) | 3.9 | 6 | N/A |
| Number of stores | 425 | 741 | 6 |

aisles. Publix also made shopping a pleasure by being one of the first supermarkets to be air-conditioned and one of the first to have automatic doors. Still today, Publix baggers take groceries to shoppers' cars for them. George Jenkins understood the concept of Easy-Est long before we ever developed our Est theory.

Despite its reputation for service, Publix isn't an upscale supermarket. Nor does it feel particularly compelled to carry the latest food fads. Publix competes with supermarkets that try to sell things cheaper, and it competes with truly upscale stores that try to match Publix's service while topping it on luxuries and high-priced merchandise. It's a real testament to Publix's bond with customers that no competitor—upscale or downscale—has been able to unseat Publix in its home markets.

We think that's because, in addition to its more obvious service elements, Publix does a number of subtle things that exemplify its customer-centricity. In its Florida stores, which tend to serve an older population, Publix makes its shelf tags larger and easier to read than those of other grocers. In addition to selling whole cakes in its bakery departments, Publix sells half cakes and quarter cakes, which are better suited for elderly couples or widows and widowers. While these kinds of things may seem insignificant, when customers consider them in concert, the message is powerful: Publix understands them. It tells customers that Publix puts them first, and that's what it takes to win at Easy-Est.

We believe it's no coincidence that both Publix and Container Store are private companies. Both also make *Fortune*'s Top 100 list of best places to work. Publix, in fact, is partly owned by its employees. Families recruit relatives and friends—it is not unusual for a dozen members of a family to work for the chain. These are people-oriented enterprises, and that helps Publix and Container Store treat their customers well.

One of the great jokes in the retail industry is that while many retailers spend gobs of money to design beautiful stores with plush ambience, that ambience makes an abrupt stop at the back room—where the employees dwell. There, the ambience is usually cement floors, cramped and dirty break rooms, and tiny employee lockers. (It's a great joke because it's both sad and true.)

The message to retail employees is plain. Customers are important; retail employees are not. How can a retailer then expect its employees to convey a positive image of the retailer to customers? How well can the employees express the notion that the retailer cares about people? Easy-Est stores seldom have this problem, because they are people-focused—meaning they take good care of customers *and* employees. Publix, as you can imagine, maintains beautiful back rooms and break areas.

We got to know Publix well in the late 1980s and early 1990s when we helped the company develop three different prototype stores in preparation for moving into the Atlanta market. That was the first time Publix opened stores outside of its home state of Florida.

It didn't take us long to recognize that Publix was something special. Immediately, one of our goals was to make sure that any new element or prototype would not hinder Publix's culture and dedication to customer service. To put it simply, our plan was this: Don't mess with Est.

Instead, we looked for ways to enhance Publix's merchandising and presentation. In Est terminology, we were looking to raise the bar for Publix in the Hot-Est category by introducing more take-out, grab-and-go food. We also positioned the fresh part of the store—produce, bakery, and deli—more prominently, because these were great strengths for Publix and could be key competitive differentiators.

Publix opened its first Atlanta-area supermarket in 1992. Today, the company has more than 100 stores there, and it is the number two grocer in Atlanta with a hefty 28 percent market share. We'd like to think we had a lot to do with that, but we know better. While we do believe our efforts helped, we know that Publix wins today because of its unadulterated commitment to customer service and being Easy-Est. The smartest thing we ever did for Publix was simple: We left a good thing alone.

---

Earlier in the chapter, we spoke with great praise about Nordstrom and Saturn. By this point, we would imagine that astute readers may have challenged those examples. Both companies are still around, but neither has the luster that surrounded the brands a decade or so ago.

Nordstrom and Saturn, two of retail's most prominent Easy–Est success stories of the early 1990s, were featured in our Est model for years, but both fell off our chart in the late 1990s.

## NORDSTROM

Nordstrom, of course, for decades has been renowned for its service-oriented sales associates and its trademark piano player. In the early days of Nordstrom's astounding success, rival department stores would study its stores before Nordstrom came to their town. The inevitable conclusion—put in their own piano players. But we always tell people, "It isn't the piano player that makes Nordstrom special—it's having what the customer wants and having it in stock."

Nordstrom carries a large assortment of large and small sizes, a policy that many retailers abandoned to save costs. Unlike some department stores, Nordstrom allows salespeople to cross-sell across departmental lines—again, saving the customer time and hassle. Nordstrom also doesn't organize its stores by "designer shops" like Polo and Tommy Hilfiger. That layout mostly benefits the department store and the designers, not the customers. That's not the way customers shop these days. In terms of making shopping easy, Nordstrom has one of retail's most hassle-free return policies.

Sure, Nordstrom is known for customer service because it has wonderful people, but what made this company Easy-Est was to engineer the merchandise organization, its presentation, and the shopping experience from a customer's perspective.

What tripped up Nordstrom in the late 1990s was not that it became less devoted to customers. In fact, we believe the company still delivers some of the best customer service in all of retailing. Nordstrom did, however, institute a number of organizational changes as it rapidly expanded (e.g., centralizing some buying that was previously done on a regional basis), which may have diminished the chain's mystique. While Nordstrom excelled at certain aspects of retailing, it fell behind on implementing the systems and technologies that are critical to providing information and efficiencies.

At the same time, Nordstrom introduced new, more contemporary designs in an ill-fated bid to woo younger customers. The changes were too much for Nordstrom's existing customers, who felt as though an old family friend was deserting them. The lesson here is that while Nordstrom still maintained many of its customer service elements, the retailer came up short in terms of "having what its target customer wanted."

We're happy to report that Nordstrom appears to be firmly back on track. Still, it provides a cautionary lesson that an Easy-Est retailer needs to excel in all aspects of the business, not just in having friendly people.

## SATURN

It's a similar story for Saturn, another former client. The company, a creation of General Motors, was a natural for Easy-Est. Saturn upended the traditional car-buying experience—which is still not far removed from the days of horse trading. For one of the more expensive purchases a consumer makes, it traditionally has been one of the most difficult for a customer to understand because of some huge variables: What am I buying and what am I paying?

Many auto retailers today are still insistent in trying to control the process, hoarding information as a way of trying to maintain an unfair advantage over the customer. That's a slowly dying model, though, because all the information is available in today's magazines and on the Internet, and customers are less interested in haggling. Today, car buyers can easily be as knowledgeable as the car salesperson—or more so.

Saturn removed the haggling and hassling from the process by adopting an authentic sticker price and a one-price policy. It created a focused product line for its target customers—young people, new families, women—and developed a clear and consistent brand. In addition to doing away with haggling, Saturn became the car industry's gold standard for providing consumers a comfortable and information-rich shopping experience, including comparative information on other cars and exceptional return and guarantee policies.

Saturn also tweaked the commission structure to get rid of high-pressure sales tactics, which occur when salespeople benefit by selling cars at higher prices. All of these things make shopping at Saturn far easier than shopping at a traditional car dealer.

Thanks to its customer-centric ways, Saturn initially enjoyed tremendous success. Saturn dealerships sold more cars than other dealerships. Surveys like J.D. Powers ranked Saturn extremely high at customer satisfaction. The company's manufacturing plant churned out cars at capacity. Saturn extended its great customer service to after-purchase maintenance and service practices that were unparalleled.

Saturn took its total package of integrity right down to the manufacturing plant floor, developing an unmatched partnership with the unions to make sure that everyone in the organization had a vested interest in producing a quality product.

Saturn truly was a different kind of car company. It wasn't just an interesting marketing campaign. In turn, customers developed a real bond with Saturn. That's why 100,000 people showed up at Saturn's factory in Tennessee for a "Saturn homecoming." Customers exhibited true affection for their Saturns. It was the kind of thing many people would expect only for high-priced sports cars or lifestyle symbols like Jeep. Who would ever care deeply about a $10,000 compact car? Saturn owners.

Yet while Saturn won many converts, it eventually fell out of favor with customers because it failed to deliver new and compelling cars. Like Nordstrom, service wasn't the issue.

Saturn's problems stemmed from its product offering and from an overly narrow definition of itself. It failed to anticipate and provide what its target audience wanted.

GM positioned Saturn as a new kind of car company, and it truly was—from assembly line to showroom. But the flaw was the unspoken emphasis: Saturn was a new kind of car company *that sold inexpensive compact cars.*

What happened when a previous Saturn buyer was ready to move up to a more expensive midsize sedan? What happened when sports utility vehicles (SUVs) came into high demand? Saturn had nothing to offer, and Saturn customers went elsewhere to find the products they wanted.

While the shorthand definition of Easy-Est is to describe it as best at customer service (the customer's definition), it is key to remember that Easy-Est is an all-encompassing positioning focused on solving customers' problems. Therefore, to win at Easy-Est you have to have the right service and the right products. A former partner of ours, Al Pennington, used to explain it like this: You step into a taxi. The seats are clean and unblemished. The floors are carpeted and appear to have just been vacuumed. It even smells nice. The driver volunteers a courteous hello. He is a veritable font of information about the city, and knows several good routes to take you where you want to go. There's just one problem—his taxi has no gas.

A retailer, regardless of how great its people and how pleasant its shopping environment, can't win at Easy-Est if it doesn't have the products customers are looking for. This is the problem that dogged Saturn, which was slow to develop a midsize car or to introduce an SUV.

Part of our work for Saturn involved developing a second generation of showrooms. The biggest hurdle we had was that the showrooms were too small: They had been designed to display only three models. That, to us, typified the narrow and eventually limiting definition of Saturn.

GM is now responding to these issues. The company recently unveiled a Saturn SUV, and has begun to promote the Saturn midsize sedan as a halfway point between an everyday vehicle and an elegant one. After achieving great initial success, GM is hoping that product innovation can revitalize Saturn. We hope so, too. But we worry, because in conjunction with the new product, Saturn has also been folded back under the GM umbrella, with much less autonomy to maintain it unique Easy-Est positioning.

We believe the biggest problem was that GM didn't realize what it had. Saturn's greatest challenge going forward is to focus on product innovation without abdicating its customer-centric ways. We believe it's possible for Saturn to do both, as long as the company doesn't forget how it won by being Easy-Est.

CHAPTER SEVEN

# QUICK-EST: WINNING WITH FAST SERVICE

Does the Est model change over time? It does, driven by the simple fact that customer needs are always changing. The challenge, we believe, is understanding what that change means and whether it is sustainable or part of a temporary trend. As an example, short-term economic factors like the recession of the early 1970s brought about the introduction of generic products by retailers. These were no-name, no-label, low-quality products that served one purpose—selling needed commodities at lower costs to consumers. This served a purpose during a tough economic period, but it wasn't really sustainable when the economy recovered. Who really wants to use bad toilet paper? At the same time, there continues to be compelling evidence that a retailer could sell nonbranded products to consumers provided that they are quality products, well explained and well marketed. Private brands are a major part of a retailer's future—generics are not.

We can boast that we see more consumer research than just about any company we know. We have had the privilege of looking at research from our clients across a dizzying spectrum of retail formats: We have analyzed, conducted research for, and studied grocery stores, convenience stores, department stores, shoe stores, sporting goods stores, pawnshops, fast-food restaurants, pet food stores, direct marketers of apparel, and auto parts retailers, just to name a few.

An interesting fact began to emerge as we delved into all this research. In the past, no matter the category, customers would invariably mention factors like price, selection, customer service, in-stock conditions, and location as the key variables in choosing a store. This isn't a big surprise, and in fact correlates well to some of the basic tenets of Est theory. A surprising thing did begin to happen, however.

The currency of *time* began to show up more and more as one of the key determinants of store choice. Time didn't mean simply *location* to the consumer—though that is still a key driver in why consumers shop where they do. Another factor was at play: Saving time became a trade-off for factors like price, service, and selection.

Hasn't time always been a factor in people's lives? Absolutely. However, changes in the consumer dynamic have made the time factor more critical than ever. The increase in the number of working women and the rise of dual-income families has upended the common view of what constitutes a household. Shopping hours from 9 A.M. to 5 P.M. are not universally convenient. Shopping increasingly takes place on nights and weekends. With the Internet, the middle of the night can be a key shopping time. Not only are more people working, but they are also working longer hours and have less leisure time available. The leisure time they do have is now filled with an incredible variety of options, from hundreds of channels of TV to sporting events and movies and the like. Shopping was once America's favorite spectator sport. While many consumers still love to shop, many more simply don't have the time. Time is becoming an increasingly precious commodity in our lives.

Inherently, we always had recognized time-saving retailers in our Est model, lumping them in with our Easy-Est retailers on the

# Quick-Est: Winning with Fast Service

Est chart. This meant that McDonald's shared a place on the chart with Nordstrom, which never sat very well with our audience. While we were able to explain that these companies deliver on different facets of service, we lost some clarity in the model.

That clarity came when we added a fifth position—Quick-Est. Quick-Est retailers include chains like McDonald's and Walgreens. Many people might not consider these chains as paragons of customer service, because neither chain is renowned for having great people at the store level. But that's from a retailer's perspective. To customers, both these retailers provide a vital service: They save customers' time. (See Figure 7.1.)

We established Quick-Est because we recognize the growing importance for retailers to satisfy their customers' desire for quick service. We also felt that we should differentiate between speed-oriented service and solution-oriented service among Easy-Est retailers.

**FIGURE 7.1** Est Chart: Quick-Est Retailers

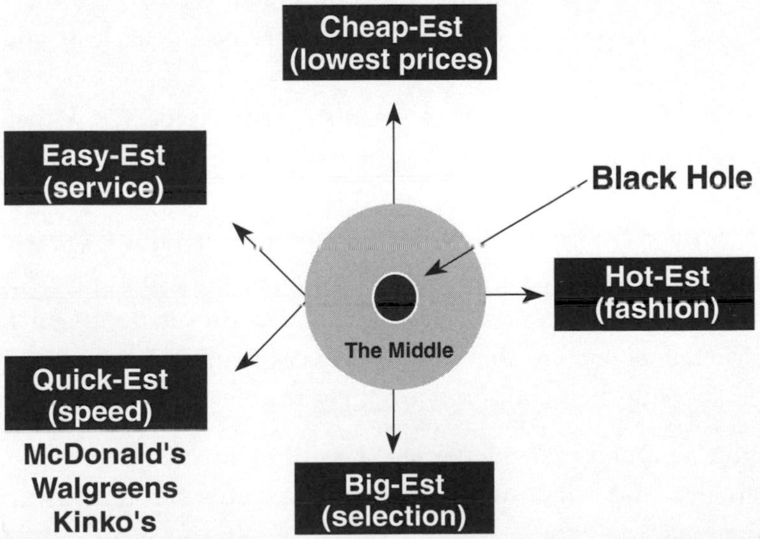

Cheap-Est
(lowest prices)

Easy-Est
(service)

**Black Hole**

The Middle

Hot-Est
(fashion)

Quick-Est
(speed)

**McDonald's
Walgreens
Kinko's**

Big-Est
(selection)

Quick-Est retailers focus on speed. They strive to be the fastest solution to satisfy a specific need.

- Quick-Est retailers have convenient locations that are easy to get into and out of. We have done a lot of work in the convenience store and gas station industries. Whether the customer is forced to turn right or left and whether there is an easy to way to get into the parking lot become key measures of convenience. There also needs to be adequate signage so consumers can see the store from a long way off.

- Quick-Est retailers have lots of locations. They understand that customers don't want to drive great distances to satisfy their needs. They are masters at understanding how small a trade area must be to qualify as truly convenient.

- They have adequate parking, close to the door. They understand that the number of footsteps to the entry is a critical component of being quick.

- Quick-Est retailers provide quick shopping. Their stores are designed for people who usually know what they're looking for and simply want to find a competent retailer that will consistently provide that product or service in the least amount of time.

- They are efficient at checkout. They understand that the greatest pet peeve of customers is waiting in line to give a retailer their money.

- Quick-Est retailers must be accurate in handling orders, and they must offer a consistent product and experience. Just as low operating costs are key for Cheap-Est retailers, Quick-Est retailers need to focus on having convenient locations and on keeping their shopping processes simple, fast, and accurate.

In short, a Quick-Est retailer looks at all elements of the shopping experience and tries to expedite the customer's total time commitment.

## Quick-Est: Winning with Fast Service

We often tell retail executives who are studying McDonald's business to forget about what's going on inside the restaurant. The real story is its drive-through, where the company does about 60 percent of its business. If McDonald's could figure out a good way to operate more than one drive-through lane per store and service those customers at peak times, that number would be even higher. Over the past five years, drive-through has been responsible for more than 80 percent of total growth in the fast-food industry.

Wendy's manages to achieve higher profits than its fast-food peers in part because its drive-throughs are among the fastest and most accurate in the industry. According to the 2001 survey of average service time done for *QSR* magazine by Sparagowski & Associates, Wendy's was the fastest drive-through, with average service time of 2 minutes, 14.7 seconds. That's far better than number two, Burger King, which managed an average time of 2 minutes, 42.2 seconds per customer. Chick-fil-A was next at 2 minutes, 47.2 seconds, followed by McDonald's at 2 minutes, 50.9 seconds. In the world of Quick-Est, seconds do indeed matter to the customer.

Drive-throughs aren't just for fast food anymore. Drugstore chains have made them a standard part of their new prototypes. Supermarkets are increasingly adding drive-through pharmacies, and even convenience stores are looking at the concept. Starbucks, which places a great deal of emphasis on the in-store experience, is aggressively adding drive-throughs to many of their locations. Even Wal-Mart has gotten into the act; drive-through windows for pharmacy services are a central part of their emerging Neighborhood Market concept. Quick may now mean never having to leave your car.

Gas stations are also innovators at Quick-Est. Pay-at-the-pump service was the big advance of the past two decades. Mobil has made what we think is the next leap forward with its SpeedPass. This is a key fob that stores a customer's credit information. It processes a transaction when waved in front of an infrared scanner at the pump or in the store. It provides self-serve at its easiest and quickest. We studied SpeedPass on behalf of a Mobil competitor, and we found that on gas purchases the fob saved a grand total of 10 seconds per transaction. How significant is 10 seconds? Ask the 6 million customers now using the SpeedPass who are probably now buying their gas only at Mobil. Anything that speeds checkout—even if it's only by five seconds—is worth telling customers about, because time wasted at checkout is one of customers' biggest gripes. SpeedPass is slowly being expanded to other venues as well. McDonald's accepts SpeedPass at selected locations and has partnered with Stop & Shop, a large regional supermarket chain in New England, to offer this payment option.

The technology behind SpeedPass may well be the biggest breakthrough in the future. SpeedPass is based on radio frequency identification (RFID) technology, which has quickly become the buzz in retail circles. Simply put, a tiny RFID chip can allow real-time tracking of a product (or person) anywhere in the supply chain. In the future, a supplier or retailer could find a single item anywhere in the supply chain (warehouse, truck, back room, grocery shelf). The implications are staggering from a supply chain standpoint and will likely represent the next revolution in retail technology. For now, we believe this technology will first show up in providing more accurate data on a warehouse-to-warehouse basis, tracking major pallets of product.

While the technology may fascinate some, our real focus is on what it will do for the consumer. Consider this: In the very near future, customers could walk into a retail store and start shopping. Using their cell phone, PDA, or a new device, they could scan an item, automatically deactivate a safety code, charge it to their credit card, and leave the store. No more lines. No more checkouts. And, for the retailer, lots of costly labor removed from the process. Today, some of this already happens, with self-scanning checkouts at the registers (another way of putting the customer in control); some stores are also experimenting with in-aisle devices. The big

# Quick-Est: Winning with Fast Service

barrier today is security: How do I know what's been paid for? With an RFID tag on an item, this problem could be solved.

Mobil and other convenience stores are Quick-Est retailers. So are retailers like Kinko's, Blockbuster, and Auto Zone. All have many features of great Quick-Est retailers, from multiple locations to no-nonsense approaches to helping customers solve their problems.

The drugstore chain Walgreens is a superb example of Quick-Est, particularly the operation of its pharmacy business. In many ways, Walgreens defined Quick-Est years before we did.

## Quick-Est: Walgreens

Walgreens top executives are a conservative bunch. They wear gray suits. They like to describe their approach to business as "crawl, walk, run." They are almost dweebish in their drugstore devotion. In fact, most of them began their careers as Walgreens pharmacists. Yet beneath that sober veneer, they've developed a corporate culture that takes bold, yet calculated risks. One of their boldest (and most successful) gambits focuses on the power of convenience and the importance of being Quick-Est. Walgreens systematically changed its operating model to draw in customers for their convenience and drugstore needs. In the process, it turned itself into one of the most consistent and successful retailers in history. (See Table 7.1.)

Walgreens was the first drugstore chain to abandon strip centers. Its competitors scoffed—they figured shoppers wanted a drugstore chain to be connected to a major anchor, like a grocery store or department store. That way, the drugstore would benefit from traffic generated by the strip mall. But Walgreens executives believed strip malls were not the best places to do business in the future—those same

129

**TABLE 7.1**   Performance of Quick-Est Retailer: Walgreens

|  | 1993 | 2002 | Compound Annual Growth Rate (%), 1993–2002 |
|---|---|---|---|
| Net sales ($ millions) | $8,295 | $28,681 | 15 |
| Net income ($ millions) | $222 | $1,019 | 18 |
| Operating profit (%) | 4.8 | 5.7 | N/A |
| Number of stores | 1,836 | 4,120 | 9 |

traffic-generating stores made it harder for their consumers to get in and out quickly. They believed customers would come to view stand-alone drugstores located at the corner of "Main and Main" as more convenient.

Essentially, Walgreens fashioned its approach after fast-food restaurants and gas stations. Stand-alone stores are easier for customers to access, and they allow customers to park closer to the door. Walgreens executives were right. Customers do prefer the convenience of such stores. That's why today, all Walgreens competitors are building stand-alone stores.

Similarly, Walgreens was the first chain to introduce drive-through pharmacies, in 1991. Again, competitors scoffed—the big profit margins in the drugstore business all come from so-called front-end products. Filling prescriptions simply gets people into the store. Drugstores make their money selling aspirin, candy bars, pantyhose, cosmetics, and contact lens solution at premium prices. Walgreens competitors figured that allowing people to pick up their prescriptions at a drive-through window would result in fewer high-margin sales. Even as veteran consultants to drive-through pioneers like McDonald's, we had our own doubts. Surely prescription drugs, with all the billing complexities and bewildering array of options, didn't mesh with a drive-through's characteristics.

Lo and behold, it resulted in more loyal customers who—whether they use the drive-through often or not—associate Walgreens with convenience. Today, about 70 percent of Walgreens' more than 4,100 stores have drive-throughs—a phenomenal fact considering Walgreens has been building them for just over a decade. Its competitors are all building drive-through pharmacy windows now, too, as are some discount stores and grocery stores. Ironically, we're not convinced that the economics of operating a drive-through make much sense. Still, we have heard from many loyal consumers (harried moms with sick kids in the middle of the night) who swear by the convenience.

Walgreens also has been a leader in technology throughout its history. It developed its own pharmacy system that interconnected with all its stores, making prescription data available throughout the chain. The system also made it possible for people to place refill orders by phone—and this was later upgraded to incorporate use of the Internet as well. After the U.S. government, Walgreens says it is the nation's largest user of satellite transmissions. Among other things, this allows for a seamless transfer of prescriptions. Ordering by phone or Internet and having your medication at the store when you get there is a powerful example of Quick-Est. The emphasis is simple, fast, and accurate. Also, knowing that you can refill your prescriptions and have pharmacists access your prescription history just about anywhere in the country is an awesome example of making life easier for customers. In the days following the 9/11 terrorist attacks, Walgreens helped more than 25,000 stranded travelers with emergency prescription needs. That's a quick and easy solution that customers will never forget. Again, Walgreens understands that a fundamental part of its business (pharmacy) goes far beyond efficiently dispensing pills—it is about building relationships with consumers that, once established, become very hard to break.

Location, of course, is the cornerstone of Walgreens' dominance at being Quick-Est. When e-commerce hysteria was at its peak, Walgreens was chided for its casual—some said sluggish—approach to developing an Internet pharmacy. Walgreens executives didn't blink. They asked, "Which is more convenient—ordering prescriptions and sundries via the Internet and waiting several days for them to arrive at your house, or stopping at one of the multiple Walgreens stores you pass on your way home from work?" Walgreens executives insisted on a "crawl, walk, run" approach to the Internet. They envisioned the Internet becoming a big part of its business, but not as a sales medium. When it comes to filling prescriptions and selling cold medicine, Walgreens' future lay in expanding its brick-and-mortar stores. As the company is quick to point out today, millions of customers now use the Internet to place a refill order on prescriptions, then pick it up in the store. This bricks-and-clicks concept makes it quicker for the customer and increases Walgreens' productivity in the process.

Unburdened by any debt, Walgreens has been one of the nation's most prolific builders in recent years. It has been abandoning strip malls for stand-alone locations, bulking up in existing markets, and simultaneously moving into new markets. During its five fiscal years from 1997 through 2001, Walgreens opened a total of 1,870 new stores. That's an average of 374 stores a year, or more than one a day. Two-thirds of the U.S. population lives within 10 miles of a Walgreens.

## Quick-Est: Winning with Fast Service

Nearly half of the population lives within two miles, which the company believes indicates that there's still plenty of demand for its stores. In downtown Chicago, Walgreens' largest market and its hometown, there are 11 Walgreens stores in a half-mile radius. In some instances, you can exit one store, look down the street and practically see the next Walgreens.

In its 2000 annual report, then-president Dave Bernauer quipped that he hadn't attended a party in two years where someone didn't ask him whether Walgreens was building stores too close together and cannibalizing its business. His answer: ". . . When we open a store very near another one, the old store usually sees a drop in sales. But in virtually every case, it builds back to its original volume and beyond. Here's the scenario: As you add stores, overall sales in the market increase, while expenses are spread over a larger base. Bottom line, profitability increases. Our most profitable markets are the ones where we've built the strongest market share." Walgreens has the leading market share in 16 of the nation's top 50 drugstore markets, and it's number two in nine of those markets. Walgreens knows that its stores can beat the Internet at Quick-Est, and that's what drugstore customers want.

Another way Walgreens wins at Quick-Est is being open whenever customers might need a drugstore. Of Walgreens' 4,100 stores, more than 900 of them are open 24 hours a day. The idea is to be available in the middle of the night in case a child is running a high fever or a spouse has an asthma attack. Walgreens plans to increase its number of 24-hour stores to 1,300 by 2006. The chain also has been remarkably successful with film development and promoting one-hour service. Remember when mall parking lots were dotted with photo-processing booths? Walgreens, capitalizing on its ultraconvenient locations, which many people drive past more often than they visit the mall or even the supermarket, realized it could be quicker. You don't see photo booths in many shopping center parking lots anymore, but you'll find photo processing in every Walgreens store.

Of course, there were some who figured Walgreens and other drugstores would be vulnerable to category killers. Remember Phar-Mor and F&M? They were significantly cheaper than Walgreens, selling many front-end items like aspirin, pantyhose, and contact lens solution at discount-store prices. Yet those stores didn't make it, because consumers looking for the cheapest price on those items were stocking up at Wal-Mart and Target. Walgreens stores rely on customers whose needs are immediate. They are ill and want to get home as soon as possible. Their pantyhose have a run. These customers, understandably, vote for convenience. They know they can find the same products cheaper at a discount store. But they trust that Walgreens will have the product in stock, and they're willing to pay extra money to save time. There's good reason why Walgreens is one of few retailers that isn't terrified by Wal-Mart, even though the massive discount store offers pharmacies in most of its stores.

In a 1998 *New York Times* article about Walgreens, then-CEO L. Daniel Jorndt told how he paced off *440 yards* from where he had recently parked his car at a Wal-Mart to get to the store's front entrance. "If you want a pack of razor blades or a stick of deodorant," Jorndt told the *Times* reporter, "the last place you want to go is a 150,000-square-foot mass merchant or the Mall of America." Today's time-pressed shoppers would rather go someplace that's Quick-Est, and that's Walgreens.

## KOZMO.COM

Kozmo.com was another brainchild of the dot-com era, and Quick-Est was clearly its game. The premise: Deliver highly consumable goods (food, video, sandwiches) to customers at their home or office within an hour. The inspiration was the fleet of messengers on bikes that efficiently deliver small packages in many metropolitan cities. In theory, Kozmo would put video rental and convenience stores out of business. What could be quicker than bringing it right to the door? A number of pizza companies (like Domino's and Pizza Hut) built billion-dollar businesses on similar premises.

In the spirit of pleasing the customer, Kozmo had a lot of positive elements in its favor. It had comprehensive selections of videos, candy, soda pop, and other convenience essentials that were competitively priced. In order to handle video returns (and generate lots of awareness), they struck a deal with Starbucks to place return boxes in their locations. Kozmo built a comprehensive web portal, introduced frequent-shopping programs, and generally spent money like many dot-coms of its era—lavishly.

What was wrong with the picture? Plenty.

We used the service occasionally at home or at the office. It was sometimes funny to order a candy bar and a coke and see our $3 order appear at the door within the hour. At home, the delivery of videos was a real plus, and we loved the convenience of not having to leave the house. From a consumer standpoint, it was hard not to like.

From a business standpoint, it was a whole different story. The costs to process an order on the Internet, pick it up at a distribution center, and send it via messenger to an individ-ual location are obviously high. How do you make up for low-dollar-amount orders with small margins? You don't, and Kozmo ultimately became a footnote in retail history.

We haven't seen any of our core Quick-Est retailers fall out of Est since we added the position in 1998, but the pitfalls are plain. Don't complicate the shopping or transaction process. Don't settle for sub-par locations that aren't sufficiently convenient for customers. Don't introduce elements that waste customers' time. Keep pursuing, devel-oping, and testing new ideas, innovations, processes, and technologies that eliminate tasks, improve accuracy, and speed up the overall process.

Our longtime client, McDonald's, has in many ways personified Quick-Est and in the process has built one of the most successful and enduring retail concepts in the world. We would be hard-pressed to find another company with greater international presence. McDon-ald's feeds more than 40 million customers a day, a staggering statis-tic, yet it has had its share of stumbles. Usually, they are related to the company moving away from its roots of Quick-Est—making sure it sells good food at a good price, *fast*. Ray Kroc understood Quick-Est when he instituted quality, service, and cleanliness (QSC) as his guid-ing principles for the company. *Quality, service,* and *cleanliness* forever remained his watchwords. (The company added a *V,* for *value,* in later years.) But to respond to changing market conditions in recent years, the company strayed from this basic formula, cluttering up the stores with promotions and cluttering up the menu with too many items. Even a new operating system was introduced that allowed for more customization of product at the expense of efficiency. In the parlance of McMillan|Doolittle, McDonald's began to mess with Mom, that core strategy that made them the most successful restau-rant operation in history.

In 2003, under new management, the company has gone back to its roots, stressing the key elements in its heritage that made it so successful. Sure, McDonald's needs to continually refine its menu and environment to meet consumers' changing needs, but it needs to do so with full respect to the Est principle that made it so successful. Recent results suggest that this back-to-the-past approach is working.

## THE FUTURE FOR QUICK-EST LOOKS BRIGHT

Quick-Est can be a core driver of a retail strategy. We don't see customers having more free time in their lives anytime soon. We expect to see more innovation in this area as retailers figure out how to save their customers time. Home delivery, drive-throughs, and digital downloads of content are all ways to deliver products in a more convenient form. McDonald's even experimented with a vending machine concept called Red Box that sold convenience items (not its food, but milk, eggs, diapers, and soda) in various locations. This was closed down, but the company is now trying the same approach with rental DVDs.

Many retailers are experimenting with smaller sizes of their units that can place them closer to the consumer. Wal-Mart, Home Depot, and Best Buy are notable for their experimentation. In the food industry, most U.S. grocers are experimenting with urban units that offer greater convenience. In the United Kingdom, Quick-Est has been taken to an all-new level in food service, with most major retailers participating, as well as their suppliers. One of the more intriguing concepts, called Rocket, was developed by Unilever, the consumer products giant. Rocket offers meals in kits sold in train stations throughout London.

Quick-Est will continue to be a key consumer driver as time becomes an increasingly precious commodity.

# CHAPTER EIGHT

# PUTTING EST TO WORK

Our representative group of Est retailers includes some of the premier retailers of today. (See Figure 8.1.) How did they get there?

One of the most common challenges we hear after giving presentations on Est retailing goes something like this: "Okay, this Est stuff looks great in theory. It seems like it does a good job of explaining why winning retailers win. But what's in it for me?" In other words, what's the application? How does Est help companies position their businesses for success?

The second most common challenge: "Isn't this a little oversimplistic? If I'm Cheap-Est, are you saying I can forgo things like selection and customer service?" Companies have a hard time believing that they can succeed with only one Est. Surely there must be companies who win by mastering one Est, two, or even three.

We agree that Est is a little simplistic on the surface—purposely so. That is the beauty of the theory: Est is memorable and helps remind retailers that winners are truly great at *one* thing in the customer's mind. It does not, however, tell the whole reason for success. As we consult with companies, it is critical to understand their situation in its complete context: their target customers, their

**FIGURE 8.1**  Est Retailers

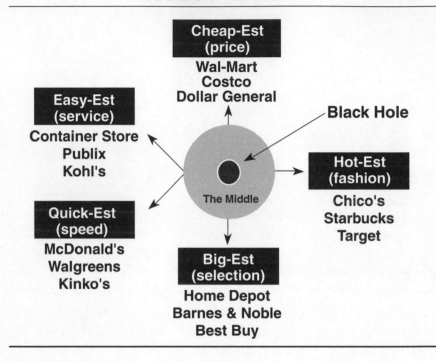

category, their competitors, and their markets. When we really get into understanding a company's current and potential positioning, we roll up our sleeves and put Est to work.

It is essential for any retailer to address each of the critical Est factors, even with a goal of not trying to dominate each one. Retailers cannot neglect any of the Est positions. Regardless of whether your stores are Cheap-Est or Hot-Est, it's essential to provide a certain degree of care to every other Est position.

## GREENS FEES, PAR, AND EST

We believe there are three basic performance levels within each Est position that can be illustrated as a bar chart. We call them Greens

Fees, Par, and Est. Greens Fees is on the opposite end of the scale from Est, and Par is right in the middle. (See Figure 8.2.)

Greens Fees is a term that golfers will recognize as the price of admission to a golf course. Greens fees may get you on the course, but they don't help you score. In retailing terms, it means that a retailer does just enough for customers to be acceptable in a given Est (selection, price, fashion, service, etc.). While it may sound negative, it really is not. Choosing to be at the Greens Fees level in a particular category is an economic decision, and it's also based on what a retailer's core customers don't want or need.

Customers don't mind that Wal-Mart is only Greens Fees level at Easy and Hot. Wal-Mart customers aren't looking for a super-pleasant shopping experience, nor are they looking for the latest fashions. They want Wal-Mart to focus its efforts on offering the lowest prices. In other words, being Cheap-Est outweighs the need to excel in certain other Est dimensions.

Similarly, customers don't mind that Costco's limited assortment makes it only Greens Fees at Big-Est. It seems to be an acceptable trade-off in order for Costco to pick the very best products (excelling at Hot-Est) at the lowest prices (Cheap-Est). Do customers make

**FIGURE 8.2**   Greens Fees, Par, and Est

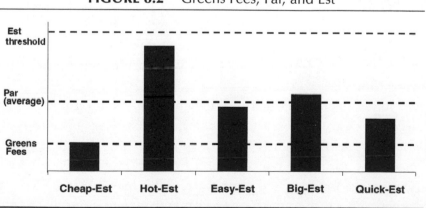

these finite equations in their heads? Most certainly not. But they do appreciate what Costco offers.

While it makes sense for some retailers to be Greens Fees at certain propositions, retailers must never fall below Greens Fees. If they do, they've fallen below the minimum accepted level and are no longer paying the price of admission. No matter how great a retailer is in other areas, if it falls below Greens Fees, customers will leave.

One prominent example of this occurred in the early 1990s, when the North Carolina–based discount supermarket chain Food Lion wound up as the subject of a television show's exposé on food safety. Although Food Lion had long been a winner at Cheap-Est, the publicity was debilitating. Food Lion had fallen below Greens Fees in an important dimension for its customers—safety. It took years for Food Lion to recover and regain customer trust.

In a different manner, Toys "R" Us fell below the customer's threshold for Easy-Est. Sure, its stores still had the biggest selection of toys, but it simply became too difficult for customers to put up with a subpar shopping experience.

Par is "pretty good," meaning a retailer is solid in that area, but not extraordinary. Retailers should be Par in areas that are important to their customers but are not *the* critical reason those customers are shopping there. Wal-Mart, for instance, is slightly better than Par at Big because its customers want the retailer to have a fairly extensive selection—even though customers are there for the low prices. With its pretty good assortment, Wal-Mart customers don't feel the need to shop at a specialty store to make sure they're not missing any major choices.

Home Depot wins at Big-Est, but another critical piece of its success is customer service. By taking good care of its customers, Home Depot is probably above Par (not quite Est, though) at Easy. This is a critical point of differentiation for Home Depot versus other home-improvement superstores, and it makes Home Depot a sharper competitor to the mom-and-pop hardware stores that thrive on convenient location and good customer service.

## Putting Est to Work

This raises another question we're asked a lot. Since Par is good (in both golf and retailing), why not try to be Par across the board? Here's why. Pursuing that kind of strategy can help you become good at a lot of things, but you will be great at nothing. In turn, your stores will stand for nothing, and eventually you will lose. There will always be a competitor that is better than you in some dimension. Customers today drive past stores that stand for nothing—even pretty good stores—to shop at Est retailers. To win over the long haul, stores must be best at something—not just good at everything. They have to meet the minimum standards (Greens Fees) in *all* areas, excel in *some* areas (Par), and be best (Est) in *one* area.

Okay, a stubborn retailer will counter, "I want to be Est at everything. We can win on all the Est dimensions. Besides, even if I don't hit them all, at least I'll be ahead on so many dimensions that it won't matter." We have to admit, this is an admirable goal and usually customer-driven. We want to give all customers the best of everything. Sounds good, but it is a practical impossibility: Can small, speed-oriented stores offer the biggest selections? Can Cheap-Est-driven retailers afford to offer the very best levels of customer service? The answer, of course, is no. Some Est dimensions are simply at odds with other ones. We don't doubt that some customers want the best of everything—but we know with certainty that retailers cannot survive trying to deliver it to them.

Great retailers—Est retailers—understand the incredibly important dynamics of these two things:

1. Targeting a particular group of customers
2. Carefully choosing what you'll be great at offering them

There is no question that the biggest ongoing challenge we have is convincing retailers that these trade-offs are not optional—they are essential to the very existence of a retailer.

In success story after success story, winners understand whom they serve and what their mission to the customer is all about. One

**145**

of our favorite retailers is Dollar General, the Tennessee-based value retail concept that is opening new units at the rate of nearly 800 per year. This company understands implicitly who its customer is (and isn't). Dollar General customers are on the lower tiers of the socioeconomic spectrum. They are often unemployed. They are primarily female. They have aspirations like all customers, but they typically don't have money to waste, living from check to check. They may only have $25 or $30 to spend on buying the essentials to feed and clothe their families, so they have to spend their money wisely. While a 24-roll pack of toilet paper at $5 at Wal-Mart is a terrific bargain, these customers may have only $1 to spend on this item in a given week. Dollar General works hard to be great at two Est dimensions: Cheap-Est (keeping prices down) and Quick-Est (being a part of the neighborhood). Why Quick-Est? Many of Dollar General's customers walk or take public transportation, so the stores need to be nearby.

Dollar General keeps prices low—real low. It brings in lots of private-label products to keep costs low, and also works with suppliers to get products at the right size and right price, every day. The stores won't win any design awards—they are basic and functional. In fact, that describes much of a Dollar General. The stores strip away much of what other retailers consider important (and indeed, so do many customers) in order to be great for their customers. This means bare-bones stores, limited advertising, and no credit card processing.

Dollar General is on a mission for its customers, and it's winning in its Est category.

Customers and economics dictate the decisions retailers might make—although retailers must start with customers first and consider economics second. Before deciding in which categories to be Par and in which to be Greens Fees, a retailer must establish how to own an Est Position. That way it will stand for something and be more valuable to today's time-starved consumers.

## APPLYING EST

Let's address the first and most important line of questioning: How can we apply all this? Est is not just some academic theory. We're not much for theories in retailing, which is more about execution and less about complex strategies. Winning at retail means executing in a gritty day-to-day business.

When we tackle retailing issues, or when retailers or service companies want to conduct this exercise themselves, here's what we suggest.

First, retailers should analyze how customers rate them at each Est position. For instance, Wal-Mart is Est at Cheap, Greens Fees at Hot, better than Par at Big, Greens Fees at Easy, and Greens Fees at Quick. This application works outside the retail world, too. We've run this exercise many times and generated extremely useful results for consumer product manufacturers. Business-to-business companies can also use this exercise, although they may want to reclassify the Est positions based on what's most important to their nonconsumer customers. For instance, we once worked with a company that operates quality-inspection labs for retailers. When performing this exercise, that company rated itself at Cheap-Est, Hot-Est (with fashion being the latest technology in product testing), Easy-Est, and Quick-Est. It dropped Big-Est (because that wasn't relevant to its customers) and added a position about integrity of service (because that's a major consideration for its customers).

An important thing to remember in doing this is that these ratings are based on *customer* perceptions, which are sometimes very different from the perceptions of senior management. It is useful, but not always necessary, to survey customers. We frequently run this exercise with groups of executives and get wildly different rankings from individual team members. When that happens, we strongly recommend surveying customers to find out what they really think. As we have pointed out often enough in this book, there are often significant differences between what a customer thinks and wants and how a retailer interprets that.

In fact, *perception* is one of our favorite words. When research indicates that customers think a store is overpriced, for example, a retailer will often counter with, "That's just their perception. In reality, we are competitively priced." In other words, the customer is wrong and the retailer is right. The [fill in the blank] customer simply doesn't know any better. We would suggest that what the customer thinks is the *only* reality that matters in retailing. If, in fact, this retailer's prices are really competitive, then there may be an issue of communication or signage. But for sure there is an issue. That's why Est exercises are always best run from the customers' point of view.

This exercise provides some good self-analysis and creates a simple visual representation depicting how customers view a company. The next step is to take a look at the competition. Rather than considering the entire retail world, as we did in introducing the Est theory, it is important to look at a defined competitive set. This competitive set often has to be defined in two distinct ways: by merchandise categories and by geography. If you're a general-merchandise retailer, you can't simply compare yourself across all categories—you need to select the ones you are specifically interested in. Say you're a retailer that happens to have sporting goods as part of your merchandise strategy. You might want to compare yourself to sporting goods generalists, sporting goods specialists, and discount chains that carry the same lines of products.

For multiline retailers, we recommend doing this exercise numerous times based on each significant category. For instance, Sears should do the Est exercise in home electronics against Best Buy, Circuit City, and local electronics stores. Sears should do the exercise again for its apparel business against J.C. Penney, Kohl's, Target, and Wal-Mart. A store like J.C. Penney would find it useful to conduct this exercise many times, breaking down its men's apparel, women's apparel, children's apparel, and home furnishings businesses against the most significant competitors in each category.

We should mention here that multiline stores like Sears and J.C. Penney should begin with a macro, whole-store perspective, before taking a category-by-category approach. An Est position can't be created from the sum of all a retailer's parts. In fact, part of the reason both of these once-mighty retailers are struggling today is that they have been unable to define themselves as a whole store. What is Sears? What is J.C. Penney? What do they stand for to customers? The power of Est is that it gives retailers a definition that consumers recognize and value.

Geography is also critical. From an immediate perspective, it is sufficient to compare yourself to the direct competitors within your market. That is who their customers are comparing that retailer against today. But be wary and conscious of what's best in class across the country (or across the world). Even if you're best in market today, it might not stay that way forever. We had the fortune to conduct strategic planning sessions for one of the premier regional grocers in the country. The company was successful, and rightly so. It clearly dominated the key Est dimensions in its market of Hot-Est and Easy-Est, but it was also smart enough to recognize that its market won't stay the same forever. The second time we ran the Est exercise, we included best in class across the country. Suddenly, the grocer's Ests weren't so strong, which gave it the sense of urgency to stay on top of its game.

Competitive rankings represent a key step. Est, Par, and Greens Fees are relative to the competition. We suggest using a peer group that includes direct and indirect competitors. Once completed, the retailer has a snapshot of its competitive universe—from the customers' perspective.

As they do when ranking themselves, retailers often have blind spots in evaluating each other. They are quick to be critical and point out what they're doing wrong and stingy with their praise.

They simply can't understand why customers would possibly go to a competitor. While competitive juices are natural, they can also obscure an objective viewpoint of the marketplace.

We recently led a study tour of prominent retail executives from around the world through the Atlanta market. One of those retailers happened to be H. Lee Scott, current CEO of Wal-Mart. Two impressions will stick with us for a long time:

1. First, he actually went on the tour, taking nearly a full day of what is obviously valuable time. Lee Scott felt that going to see retail stores was a productive use of his time. He stayed focused on the stores, not talking on his cell phone. We ran into several of his U.S. competitors at the same conference who stayed back at the hotel. They had "seen these stores before" was their reply for begging off the tour.
2. Second, Lee asked a lot of questions when touring stores of the associates (he had a practiced patience with consultants and other hangers-on). The questions were basic but revealing: What's selling? What do you like about working here? He was quick to praise the efforts of Target, one of his fiercest competitors.

For these and many other reasons, the culture of Wal-Mart is in good hands. The spirit of Sam Walton lives on—it's about the stores, the products, and the people. Lee Scott demonstrated that powerfully—a lesson his competitors should be quick to heed.

Another famous retailer, Stew Leonard, adopts a similar philosophy. When his team visits stores, they are allowed to report back only on positive ideas and praise for the competition. He instituted a One Idea club—anyone on his team could take a trip to see competition provided that they came back with one great idea. One idea can multiply in a hurry.

One cautionary note: Don't get hung up on debating whether to rank a company, say, halfway between Est and Par versus one-third of the way between Est and Par. You're splitting hairs and wasting time with such discussions. These rankings are meant to be broad and general. Don't sweat the minute details. The point is, it's easy to spot who has an Est and who doesn't. It then becomes pretty easy to spot the winners and the losers.

With this snapshot of the competitive universe, retailers can begin to get a sense of where they might want to take their business. For instance, a retailer might see that nobody in its category is Hot-Est. The retailer could explore that option, considering what it would take to be Hot-Est. What would the trade-offs be? For instance, being Hot-Est might reduce its ability to be Cheap-Est. Next, do the same analysis for each Est position, keeping in mind that some Est positions may not be feasible and some may not be important to customers. Also, this should be done in the context of the competitive universe and with consideration of the retailer's own internal strengths and weaknesses. Even if Hot-Est were available, perhaps the retailer lacks keen fashion spotters and has no capacity for moving products quickly. In that case, Hot-Est would not be such a hot idea for that retailer.

In addition to trying to discover a suitable Est position, keep Par and Greens Fees in mind. We've seen many times where a company doing this exercise realizes that being Par in one area offers a key differentiation point that could be used to expand certain lines of business. We believe this is how the exercise gets from ethereal positioning or branding to thinking about market niches and growth opportunities.

Essentially, the Est exercise helps a retailer to analyze how it rates with customers at each Est position, and then to consider what it would take to alter those positions. Further, it provides the key external context: What's important to customers? Where's the competition?

Performing this exercise won't result in a course of action. But it's a great thought starter for strategic discussions. It helps answer: Where are we today with customers? Where can and should we go to win in the future? Last, it provides a graphic illustration that a retailer can revisit to see whether it has succeeded in moving the needle and made its stores Greens Fees, Par, and Est in all the right places.

The final piece of an Est exercise is to complete the reality check (where we are today) and then also plot out the future. What would the ideal future state look like? If we did pursue this Est, what would have to change to make it happen and what would our organizational and capital needs look like? Est can provide a road map to follow in the future and a fast and effective grading tool to see whether progress is being made.

## EST IN THE REAL WORLD

One of the real-world challenges faced by retailers or suppliers: What can actually be done to transform a business? They may understand the Est theory, buy into its basic premise, but still be unable to create meaningful change within the organization. This tends to be the result of several factors:

- *They are past the retail inflection point.* In many instances, the companies simply failed to react in time to the changes that were occurring within the marketplace. The inflection point passed them by and customers simply gave up or the economics became so daunting that no amount of change could save them. Toward the end of Montgomery Ward and Service Merchandise's retail life, the valiant efforts of management simply were not enough to overcome the repeated poor decisions and failures to act of the past.
- *Competition may have Est covered.* It does happen every once in a while that there simply is no clear position to move toward. The competition may be too good and too strong to find an

# Putting Est to Work

Est. Consider the dilemma of Kmart's current management. They have inherited a company that was poorly run and failed to react to the market signals of the past 20 years. The store base is tired and still struggles with the basics of retail execution. Even more critically, they face two spectacular competitors—Wal-Mart and Target—who have created very strong Est positions. Wal-Mart is dominating on Cheap-Est and continues to strengthen its assortments. Target owns Hot-Est and is pushing hard on Easy-Est. Quick-Est, the remaining Est, may not be achievable in a big-box setting—that distinction may belong to the dollar stores that have many more locations with smaller footprints. Where does Kmart go? That is the billion-dollar question with no easy answers. If there is a solution, it will be driven by finding a particular set of target customers whom the competition is not addressing and developing an Est for them. A bright spot: Kmart seems to be better positioned to reach an ethnic consumer. That may represent its salvation.

- *Change must be dramatic.* Finally, retailers may think they're changing, but customers often don't see those changes. Customers don't make a habit of walking into every retail store every day to see what's new. They typically have their minds made up about where they're going to shop, so change needs to be dramatic and jarring. We are amazed at how many focus groups we attend only to see the customers play back a retailer's brand strategy of 10 years ago. Even more frustrating for retailers (and the consultants who try to create that change) is how little customers notice even when they do shop the store. Even the most loyal customers often miss whole departments of merchandise as well as new fixtures and signage. The reason is simple: Customers are very focused when they shop—they typically do not care about most of the messages we are bombarding them with.

## EST IN ACTION: BEST BUY AND COACH

Can Est really work to transform a company? Yes, although it may not be very easy. When it does work, the results can be phenomenal.

Best Buy was a struggling regional electronics chain in the late 1980s. Like many of its peers, it was able ride the tremendous technology wave to develop a decent-sized regional chain. When the technology cycle slowed, Best Buy was in trouble. Sales were slowing, margins were dropping, and the best of the regional chains at the time—Circuit City—was aggressively moving into its markets. Competitors were going out of business at a fierce rate and there was a laundry list of failed competitors. It is almost certain that Best Buy would have made that list if it hadn't attempted radical change.

Best Buy's solution was initially called Concept II, which opened in Rockford, Illinois, in the early 1990s. Best Buy made some radical changes in their store:

- Gone were commissioned salespeople, which had been a staple at Best Buy and most of its competitors' establishments. These were the hard-selling employees who tried to convince customers to buy more expensive items and higher-margin brands. These employees had also been desperate to sell extended service contracts, which typically make more money for a retailer than the actual product itself.
- Product was stacked on the floor for customers to pick up and buy. This changed the transaction cycle, which previously had often involved the customer having to visit three separate areas in the store: the salesperson, the payment desk, and the loading dock.
- New products were added to the mix. The most radical idea was the introduction of consumable media products—compact disks, videos, video games, and computer software.

154

# Putting Est to Work

Best Buy embraced the radical idea that these products would drive more traffic into the stores—customers do not buy refrigerators and televisions very often.

- Computers also became a big part of the business. Best Buy jumped into this category in a major way at just the right time. It offered lots of sales but very low margins.
- These new stores were much larger in size to accommodate new products and to move the back room to the sales floor.

What happened was fascinating. Sales jumped instantly while gross margins plummeted. Those extended service contracts all but disappeared when consumers were no longer pressured to buy them. Best Buy clearly had a hit on its hands with consumers, but still faced a very difficult task of making its model profitable. The company was able to convince consumers of Cheap-Est and began to develop a secondary position as Big-Est, which is far better developed today.

Best Buy began to engage in a race to get its SG&A down faster than gross margins. At several points in its history, it was questionable whether Best Buy would achieve that. In 1996, for example, sales had more than doubled from four years earlier, to nearly $7.7 billion. Unfortunately, net margins and return on equity had declined to nothing. In other words, this company came very close to going out of business, largely because of internal issues like inventory controls.

The company came roaring back afterward, finally perfecting both the consumer model and the business drivers needed to make money. While never abandoning its initial Ests, Best Buy recognized the need to improve the experience (Easy-Est) and dramatically elevated its position as a provider of new products—first to embrace new technologies like DVD and digital product, then to become a hip place to shop, particularly for younger consumers, by using memorable and slightly irreverent advertising.

The repositioning has worked. After teetering on the edge of the

Black Hole in 1996, the company has steadily improved sales, operating margins, net margins, and return on equity. In 2001, Best Buy reached more than $20 billion in sales on over 20 percent compounded annual growth during the past decade. It produced a 3.0 percent net margin, excellent in an industry known for notoriously slim profits, and delivered a 22 percent return on equity. Not bad for a struggling regional chain that almost didn't make it. Best Buy slumped somewhat in 2002, but recovered significantly in 2003. (See Table 8.1.)

Coach's story is equally impressive, though it was not as terrifyingly on the brink of oblivion. The respected leather goods company, once a division of Sara Lee, was known for making high-quality leather handbags. Tan-colored leather handbags, to be more specific. The company had a nice little niche and certainly made a great product. How, then, did it transform itself into one of the hottest suppliers and retailers? By embracing the power of Hot-Est.

Coach's management team realized that in order to sell more products, the company had to become more relevant in customers' lives. This meant selling more products to existing Coach customers and reaching new customers as well. The company developed new product designs, introduced bright new colors, and even began to branch out of leather and experiment with new materials.

**TABLE 8.1**   Est in Action: Performance of Best Buy

|  | 1993 | 2002 | Compound Annual Growth Rate (%), 1993–2002 |
|---|---|---|---|
| Net sales ($ millions) | $3,007 | $20,946 | 24 |
| Net income ($ millions) | $41 | $99 | 10 |
| Operating profit (%) | 2.6 | 4.8 | N/A |
| Number of stores | 151 | 679 | 18 |

The product line expanded as well, even to dog collars. To use the latest buzzword, Coach moved from being a seller of products to being a lifestyle brand.

Dramatic change, to be sure, but how did the company communicate that to the consumer? It is notoriously difficult for a brand to introduce new products as a wholesaler when the retailers for that brand may have liked it just fine as a limited resource.

Coach's solution was to develop high-profile concept stores—not the gaudy flagship stores that make headlines and lose money, but profitable enterprises. Coach runs outlet stores as well, and retail accounted for 62 percent of its nearly $1 billion in sales in 2002. Coach has produced stunning numbers—net margins higher than 15 percent, with gross margins exceeding 70 percent. That's the power of Hot-Est.

# PART III
# The Future

# CHAPTER NINE

# EST ISN'T FOREVER

## Retail Is Tougher Than Ever

Probably the biggest problem with any theory isn't the theory itself—it's the examples that are used to prove the point. With a great degree of certainty, we know that just about any retailing example we use to prove the Est theory will inevitably run into some difficulties. Even in the course of writing this book, we have seen some great retail companies hit relatively hard times (The Gap and Home Depot) and others that have bounced back nicely. It seems that any example becomes obsolete almost before the ink dries.

This doesn't mean Est isn't valid; it simply means that something happened to those retailers, whether internally or externally driven, that caused them to fall off our charts. While we have had some fairly stunning examples of enduring retail success (Walgreens and Wal-Mart spring to mind), we've also had some shining stars fade. If they haven't made it to the Black Hole, they're undoubtedly swimming in the Sea of Mediocrity. Est isn't forever—the customer and the marketplace see to that.

When retail chains fail and wind up in the Black Hole, the media invariably cites increased competition as part of the reason. Of course, more competition is a fact of every business these days. The explosion in new retail stores over the past three decades has been unprecedented. For every man, woman, and child in this country, there is now about 21 square feet of retail space, according to the International Council of Shopping Centers. That's nearly three times as much as there was in 1972, when there was only 7.9 square feet of retail space per capita. (See Figure 9.1.)

In the past decade, retailers, mall developers, and business reporters constantly have asked, Is America "over-stored"? It is a tough question to answer. Even though 21 square feet of retail for every American sounds like a monstrous figure and makes for a great factoid in speeches, perhaps the world's most powerful consumer citizenry could support more—maybe 30, even 40 square feet of retail space per person.

Real estate development, whether homes, offices, condos, or shopping centers, generally follows a predictable pattern. Developers build until they've built too much. The unfortunate developers who build when there's already too much learn that the market is

**FIGURE 9.1**   Retail Space per Capita

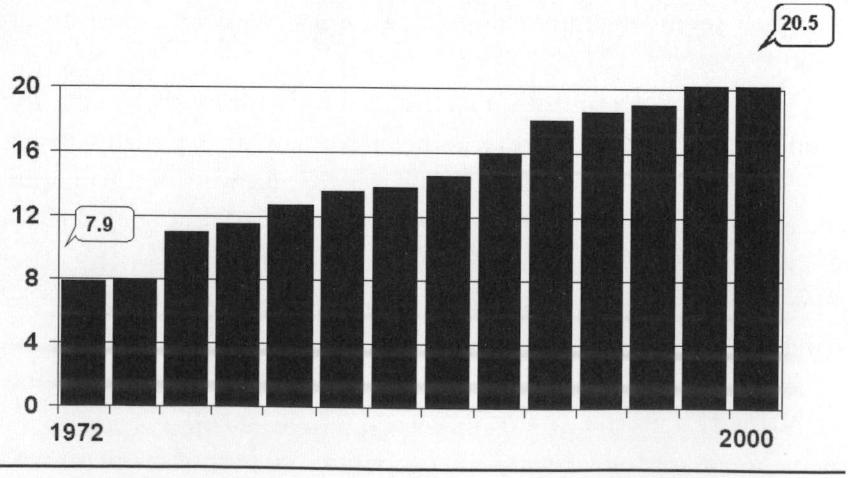

overbuilt when their homes, offices, condos, or shopping centers sit vacant or half constructed. Then they take a financial beating.

As the 1990s came to a close, we believe the data showed that, yes, America had reached the point of having too many stores and too much retail space. The first evidence was the increase in retail bankruptcies. When there are too many competitors, some must go. The second piece of evidence came from a slowdown in retail productivity, which retailers measure in sales per square foot. Amazingly to us, despite technological advances, scientific retailing, and sophisticated marketing, sales per square foot in this country has actually declined. It has been declining at a fairly steady rate for a long period of time. We're building more stores and becoming less efficient in the process. To us, the combination of these two facts proves that America has reached the point of being "over-stored." (See Figure 9.2.)

Some would argue, so what? As long as retailers are increasing their profitability, who really cares if sales per square foot is declining? Isn't it really all about profitability in the final analysis? To

**FIGURE 9.2**   Retail Sales per Square Foot

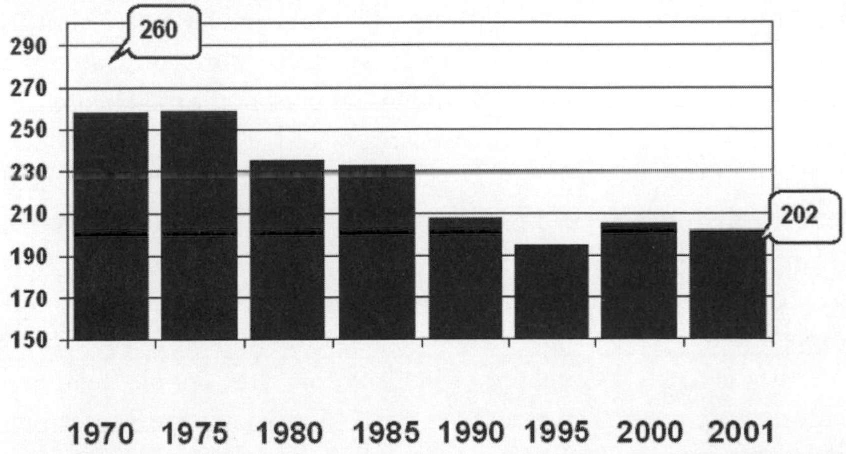

respond, we turned to a final measure to understand retail perform-ance. While there are literally hundreds of measurements to assess on a retailer's balance sheet, the one we like the best is *earnings power*. This takes into account two key variables: *margin,* a measure of prof-itability, and *asset utilization,* which accounts for how efficiently a retailer uses assets like inventory. Again, the numbers reveal that earnings power has slowed or declined for all but the truly power-house retailers. For 2002, those powerhouse retailers (i.e., retailers who produce more than 10 percent earnings power and who have increased earnings power from year to year) include Auto Zone, Bed Bath & Beyond, Dollar General, Dollar Tree, Kohl's, Kroger, Lowe's, Pacific Sunwear, Ross Stores, Safeway, Target, Tuesday Morning, Walgreens, Wal-Mart, and Whole Foods. In case anyone is wondering, the retailers who have managed to steadily increase earnings power also happen to be predominantly Est retailers. Sur-prise, surprise.

Not only are there more stores, but there are better stores. The stores that expanded the most in the past three decades are also the ones still winning with customers today—stores like Wal-Mart, Target, Home Depot, Lowe's, and Walgreens. While expanding their geographic reach, these retailers were also simultaneously rais-ing customer expectations. Customers today have far better choices than they have ever had. Spectacular specialty stores now rule the malls, with wonderful products and visual presentations. The gener-alists (variety stores, department stores, and general-merchandise catalogs and stores) are fading and being replaced by bigger and better stores. We often take international retailers on study tours, organized trips to study the best U.S. formats. Their mouths literally drop to see the choices (and great prices) available to U.S. con-sumers. The average supermarket in the United States now carries over 40,000 stockkeeping units (SKUs), more than double the num-ber of a little more than a decade ago. A Wal-Mart supercenter car-ries well over 100,000 SKUs. The United States is a consumer's paradise, and customers have become accustomed to stunning choices. Once customers raise their expectations, they don't lower them again to previous levels. While raw retail square footage has increased by nearly three times over the past 30 years, competition has actually increased fivefold over that period.

There's no greater pressure on retailers today than keeping up with sharp, well-financed, expansion-minded competitors. Decades ago, when American retail was dominated by generalists like Sears, Montgomery Ward, and Kmart, the competition wasn't very good. Case in point: One of Ward's great claims to fame was that it allowed catalog customers to return items at no expense. That was innovative, because at that time many merchants either didn't accept returns or charged customers for them. Sears didn't accept credit cards other than its own until the early 1990s. Imagine a retailer today with those kinds of policies? Customers would laugh them out of business.

From apparel to toys to TVs, in previous decades people had far fewer choices. Highly focused specialty stores didn't exist, and customers came to accept that they'd simply have to try their luck at several generalists to find what they needed. Those days are long gone, because in retail today the competition is unrelenting and unforgiving.

## CONSOLIDATION

As competition intensified and the rush to expand heightened, retailers began consolidating. Winning retailers bought from a position of strength, while others sold out because of weakness or, in some cases, desperation: A buyout was the only way for their stores to survive. We've been tracking retail consolidation since McMillan|Doolittle's formation in 1986. In every category, there's been a steep increase in the amount of market share dominated by fewer players, and we believe there's much more to come.

**TABLE 9.1**   Consolidation in Key Retailing Segments

| | Market Share of the Top Three Retailers* | | | |
| --- | --- | --- | --- | --- |
| | 1986 (%) | 1996 (%) | 2000 (%) | 2002 (%) |
| Department stores | 39 | 60 | 71 | 82 |
| Discount stores | 61 | 77 | 84 | 86 |
| Building materials | 11 | 31 | 39 | 42 |
| Consumer electronics | 15 | 34 | 35 | 37 |
| Drugstores | 18 | 33 | 42 | 43 |
| Supermarkets | 18 | 14 | 28 | 27 |

*Sales of the three largest retailers in each segment as a percent of total sales in that segment.

Source: © 2003 National Research Bureau.

Retail stores developed in the United States as regional businesses, and there are still relatively few national players. In categories like home electronics, drugstores, and sporting goods, we're still at the point of regional chains bumping into each other as they aspire to expand nationwide. American retail remains far less consolidated than that of other developed nations, but the trend in the United States has been steadily heading toward greater consolidation. For instance, in 2002, the top three department store chains had 82 percent market share. That's up from 60 percent in 1996 and 39 percent in 1986. The top three discount store chains, meanwhile, had 86 percent market share in 2002 compared with 61 percent market share in 1986. (See Table 9.1.)

## COMPRESSED LIFE CYCLE

While retail stores have been consolidating, we've also seen the life cycle for stores being squeezed. In the past, the retail life cycle has looked like a typical bell curve: a period of development for an emerging concept, followed by a period of rapid growth, then maturity as the curve flattens, and eventually decline. That cycle still exists, of course, but it's been significantly compressed as new retail concepts grow, mature, and decline faster than ever.

Think about the history of these retail formats: peddlers, mom-and-pop stores, variety/five-and-dime stores, department stores, category killers, and e-commerce. Peddlers, of course, have been around for more than 500 years, but for the past 50 years the prominence of peddlers has been in decline. Mom-and-pop stores have been around for more than 300 years. They dominated the landscape before our nation's founding, and held that position well into the mid-1900s. Today they are in precipitous decline. Variety stores like Woolworth and Ben Franklin were the nation's first mass retailers, but they are dead now, after only about 50 years of existence. Department stores are also about 50 years old, and now are clearly in a state of decline. Discount stores were hatched 40 years ago. In just 40 years they've reached a level of maturity where even the nation's number three discount store, Kmart, is fighting for survival. Meanwhile, the leaders Wal-Mart and Target have both become grocers as a way to continue expanding. The category-killer sector, including stores like Home Depot and Toys "R" Us, is about 20 years old, and already category killers are mature, perhaps even declining. E-commerce retailing, with all its hype and irrational exuberance, matured in a matter of a few years, and many upstarts were quickly forced out of business. (See Figure 9.3.)

The cycle is compressing in part because of the globalization of communications. Ideas can spread almost instantaneously, thanks to mediums like the Internet. While good ideas once were able to remain regional and somewhat obscure, that's no longer the case. Ideas and best practices now spread internationally, often in a matter of days, as traditional barriers and borders begin to disappear.

The other big squeeze on life cycle is the high-risk, high-reward influence of venture capital and public markets. Retailers have greater access to funds than they did in the past, from both private and public sources. However, that money comes with strings

**FIGURE 9.3**   Compressing Retail Life Cycle

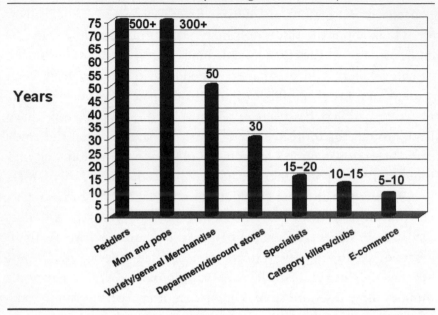

attached—the expectation of fast growth. As e-commerce showed, the battle for first-mover advantage and critical mass has often become the top priority. Getting there first, with a sufficient number of stores to support marketing efforts and internal infrastructure (regional managers and the like), requires a concept to move fast. The result is a compressed retail life cycle that forces new concepts to come of age quickly. It also puts pressure on older formats and established retailers to innovate or risk idly sitting by while a fast-moving new concept takes away customers.

We think a couple prime examples of the high-risk, high-reward pressures fueling retail growth and life-cycle compression are Gap's Old Navy chain and Pets.com, one of many upstarts to wind up in the e-commerce Black Hole.

In the late 1990s, Old Navy was hailed as one of the great retail success stories of the decade—with good reason. The chain, which featured Gap-style clothes at discount-store prices, was intended to reach younger customers and more budget-conscious families than did Gap. Originally, Gap wanted Old Navy stores to do $350 in sales per square foot. The stores blew the top off that goal, producing a whopping $500 in sales per square foot. Gap had a real winner. In less than four years, Old Navy surpassed $1 billion in revenue, making it the fastest-growing retailer ever. Its store count ballooned from 59 in 1995 to 842 in 2003, and while the first Old Navy stores were small, its newer stores were getting progressively larger, even up to 40,000 square feet, which is roughly half the size of a Kmart store.

Eventually, though, as its popularity and its newness faded, Old Navy stores became less productive. The stores, now opening in malls right next to Gap stores, were cannibalizing Gap and Banana Republic sales. With its big stores, Old Navy became less nimble and less able to rebound from fashion missteps. Plus, the higher costs of operating such big stores changed the financial model.

What's interesting is that Old Navy is still making close to $350 per square foot in sales. But that number is no longer as viable because of the accelerated expansion. We believe a big factor fueling the overexpansion, which is at the root of Old Navy's problems today, was pressure from public investors. The Gap has Old Navy firmly back on track to becoming a great item merchant. We believe that slower growth would have been more sustainable and offered fewer bumps along the way.

Pets.com was a bad idea from the start, and it was poorly executed, to boot. People who truly believed in Pets.com—and we can't help wondering whether the believers were actually banking on an e-mania surge in the stock price rather than the long-term viability of the company—had to disregard a lot of bad signs. Pet food and supplies is a category that's driven by consumables, things like dog food and cat litter. These are things that people most often buy when they need them, meaning they're unable and uninterested in waiting a few days for delivery. These items are also large and heavy, making them expensive to ship, and they have relatively low profit margins. Even the more profitable supply items, such as collars, shampoos, bowls, and beds, are driven by the consumables business, because people tend to buy these things when they're at a pet store, discount store, or grocery store replenishing their supply of dog food or cat litter.

Another warning indicator that the believers and e-crazy investors overlooked: market size. With sales of roughly $18 billion per year, pet food and supplies is a good-sized business. Investors were correct in assuming that an increasing portion of that business will move online. Even a generous estimate would put 5 percent of that total business online 10 years from now. That's roughly a $1 billion market. Say the leader can nab 25 percent of that, and you've got a $250 million company that can maybe manage a 5 percent margin, for annual profits of $12 million. That could be a nice business, and our bet is that there will be plenty of successful business opportunities in numerous categories like that in the future—and none of them will have TV commercials in the Super Bowl.

Pets.com was just one example of too much hype, too much investment, and too many unrealistic expectations about how fast consumers will adopt shopping online. Had Pets.com moved slower and invested an amount commensurate with the market it was chasing, perhaps the company could have made it. Instead, the only major value left when the pieces of Pets.com were auctioned off was its sock puppet spokesdog—and a lesson for other retailers about the compressed life cycle of e-commerce.

Life cycles are shrinking so dramatically that it's nearly gotten to the point where investors, retailers, and retail suppliers should begin to view stores the same way investors view dance clubs or trendy restaurants. Those types of businesses are notorious for being big moneymakers for two or three years, then either limping along for a time or simply going away. The investment strategy is to get in fast, make lots of money, then get out. While retail may never move quite as fast as hip restaurants and nightclubs, the lesson is plain: In today's market, stores must be extremely successful quickly.

## THREE'S A CROWD

While studying consolidation and market share trends, we've always looked at the top three retailers in a category. In coming years, we may have to narrow our scope to the top two chains for a more accurate picture. That's because in retail these days, three's a crowd.

Life ain't easy for the number three retailer in a category. Just ask Kmart or OfficeMax. Try to name the number three retailer in pet stores, sporting goods, or home electronics. We all know General Electric's mantra about being number one or number two in all of its businesses. Well, GE wasn't even close with its one retail holding—Montgomery Ward. Consequently, in early 2001 the company that "brings good things to life" decided it was Black Hole time for Montgomery Ward.

Part of the reason that three's a crowd is the growth and maturity of the Big-Est retailers, the category killers. Pressured to grow by public or private investors, the category killers forged into each other's markets. The competition drove prices down, profits inevitably followed, and the weaker chains couldn't survive.

Think of home-improvement superstores. In addition to industry leaders Home Depot and Lowe's, there used to be Home Base and Builders Square, but both those chains failed in recent years. Now the industry is dominated by Home Depot and Lowe's, two giant, publicly held companies. The number three spot (a *very* distant third) is occupied by a privately held, little-known company called Menards, which has stores in nine upper-Midwest states, from Indiana to North Dakota.

## FALLING OUT OF EST

How do retailers lose an Est position? There are three classic patterns:

1. *New competition.* During the Est exercise, we mentioned that competition truly has to be accounted for on a local level. Customers shop the stores in their trade areas. Retailers simply have to be the best in their marketplace to succeed. In the absence of better competition, a retailer can be an Est for its market, temporarily. Before Wal-Mart came to many rural American markets, the customer's best option was to shop from catalogs, frequent smaller retail establishments, or visit places like Western Auto, which sold a variety of general-merchandise products. One of our first clients was a company called Otasco (Oklahoma Tire and Supply Company), which sold automotive products, sporting goods, and hardware. The strategy for a while was to close up shop when a Wal-Mart came to town. Running away didn't work in the long term, and Otasco joined other retailers who had unceremoniously tumbled into the Black Hole. For many regional chains that existed in the United States, the same held true. Regional discounters such as Ames, Bradlees, Caldor, Venture, and Jamesway eventually were sucked into the Black Hole when better Est players like Wal-Mart and Target made it to their markets.

2. *Rising Est levels.* Sometimes, a new competitor enters the market and changes the very nature of Est. A company may indeed have achieved Est only to see a new competitor change the standard. Est levels have been rising—and it's tougher than ever to maintain an Est position. Take the book industry. A standard book-retailing store until the late 1980s was around 5,000 square feet and carried about 15,000 titles. In larger markets, there would typically be a downtown store that would have authoritative selections. For real selection, a customer would have to

visit a local library. When Barnes & Noble and Borders began building 20,000-square-foot superstores in suburban locations, Est standards suddenly changed. These stores carried 10 times the amount of books, in a beautiful retail setting, and the Est bar was forever raised, not just on Big-Est, but also on a key dimension of Easy-Est. Fast-forward about a decade and along comes Amazon.com, which offers literally millions of books online. Suddenly, Big-Est could no longer be achieved in a physical setting, and Est was again forever changed. Fortunately, the big booksellers like Barnes & Noble have created a powerful component of Easy-Est, with today's modern bookstore replacing the library, coffee shop, and singles bar, on occasion, in many communities. Also, many great independent bookstores have capitalized on Hot-Est, offering just the right assortments for their communities or focusing on a key category (kids' books, spirituality) to differentiate themselves.

3. *Eye off the ball.* Of course, some companies fall out of Est in an entirely self-inflicted manner. They simply lose track of what their customers need in a shopping experience. Companies like Toys "R" Us and Home Depot, we would argue, lost track of what was important to their customers, allowing competition to enter their markets. Currently, many of the major grocery chains in America are struggling to maintain sales as they lose business to Wal-Mart and focused specialists. Sure, competition is a factor, but failure to react to the trends that surround them is the greater sin.

## MARKET SQUEEZE

Customers are part of this market squeeze, too. Technology has made modern life increasingly fast-paced. That means consumers' needs, desires, and shopping behavior change quicker as well. What is okay for shoppers today is likely to be insufficient in the near future. Customers have become increasingly unwilling to forgive retailers or to wait around for floundering stores to improve. Customers simply don't have to deal with incompetent merchants anymore, because they have so many other options. Today's fast-changing, increasingly demanding customers are further squeezing the market. This escalates the importance of stores being customer-centric. It is more important than ever for stores to be constantly adapting and testing new prototypes.

The end result of all this pressure from competitors, customers, and investors is a viselike squeeze on the market such as retailers have never before experienced. We're destined to see more retail bankruptcies, more going-out-of-business sales, and more consolidation in the future. When you also consider the trend that many people want to spend less time shopping, the implication is clear. Pretty good isn't good enough anymore. Consumers don't want more stores, and they don't want more retail square footage. They want more Est retailers.

# CHAPTER TEN

# DEVELOPING TOMORROW'S HOT IDEAS

Yes, retail is a mature business. Yes, America is "over-stored." But that doesn't diminish the importance of innovation. To the contrary, retail innovation is more critical than ever because of the market squeeze caused by increased competition, investors' appetite for growth, and customers' increasing demands for efficiency. Retailers must develop hot new ideas—or at least borrow them from somebody else—to ensure future retail success.

Yet the tone of this book suggests that it is going to be tougher to develop the next hot idea in an intensely competitive market. Simply and unfortunately put, most new ideas fail. In this chapter, we delve into the genesis of hot ideas—where they're coming from and how they can survive.

From McMillan|Doolittle's standpoint, nothing is more exciting than being handed a blank piece of paper and asked to help develop a new retail concept. We have been involved in some great successes and some notable failures. Clearly, the process makes our creative juices flow. That's why we were particularly disappointed when the calls to help develop new concepts started to slow down in the late 1990s.

The brief hysteria over e-commerce in the late 1990s resulted in an almost complete hiatus in the development of new retail concepts and prototypes. For a couple years, venture capitalists wanted to invest only in Internet-related retailers, and many established companies devoted large amounts of money to developing e-commerce web sites—at the cost of new store development. With e-mania behind us, now is the time for retailers to develop new concepts. While we remain passionate about the need for multichannel solutions, brick-and-mortar stores are here to stay. At the very least, retailers should be rethinking and reenergizing their existing formats.

## THE HOT ZONE

Tomorrow's hot ideas are predictable if retailers pay attention to the right trends. The key to realizing and developing a hot idea is to correctly assess three things: the needs of customers, the competitive environment, and the retailer's own internal strengths and weaknesses.

What we call the Hot Zone is where many of tomorrow's hot ideas germinate. It lies at the intersection of correctly responding to consumer trends, determining a retailer's capability of delivering on a strategy, and finding a market position defendable against the competition. (See Figure 10.1.)

Consider Target, the self-proclaimed "upscale discounter." Target tapped into a consumer trend by realizing that even wealthy and middle-income shoppers would flock to discount stores. Rather than selling dowdy (and cheaper) products, which was the staple of most discounters, Target decided to sell these customers trend-right, fashion-forward merchandise. Target was able to accomplish this extraordinary merchandising feat because it leveraged heavily from the internal strengths of its parent company, which operated high-fashion department stores. Target's culture understood and embraced fashion. Finally, Target hit a defensible market position because Wal-Mart and Kmart were content to attract customers with low prices, opting for

# Developing Tomorrow's Hot Ideas

**FIGURE 10.1**   Retailing's Hot Zone

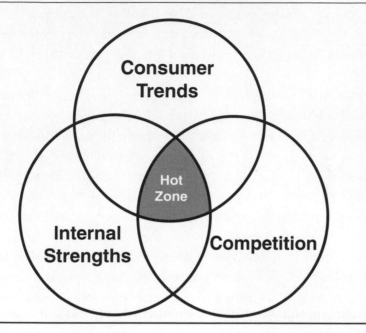

inexpensive goods rather than fashionable merchandise. Target hit the bull's-eye of the Hot Zone. Not surprisingly, it has become a spectacularly successful retailer, even when held up to the most extraordinary retailer in history, Wal-Mart.

Coming up with the concept for a hot idea is just the beginning. For a hot idea to succeed, a store must simultaneously meet consumer needs, be easily understood, and be operated profitably. Achieving this is the great challenge—and the great thrill—of creating a new retail concept.

It requires retailers to be diligent students of consumer trends. How do they behave now? Why? How will they behave in the future? Why? How does this concept benefit specific customers?

To become a hot idea, a new concept must first solve a real

problem for consumers. Are there enough consumers out there to support the new proposition? Too many new concepts are conceived to solve problems for the retailers—to foster growth or expand a fast-growing division or one that is the CEO's pet project.

After determining how it helps consumers, the retailer can figure out how to communicate the store's proposition. Great concepts (Est concepts) are easily understood because they are built on a compelling proposition. Far too often, we see new concepts that try to straddle lots of potentially intriguing ideas but succeed at none. The Black Hole is never very far behind.

Finally, the retailer must figure out how to deliver on that proposition with acceptable profits. Developing an acceptable economic model is always harder than it appears. It takes years and many prototypes to develop the right size, the right labor mix, the right merchandise assortments, the right amount to spend on construction and buildout, the right message to the consumer, and so on. Far too often, new retail concepts are shelved because the parent company ran out of time, money, or patience (sometimes all three). We cannot emphasize this last point enough. There are precious few examples of concepts that are big winners out of the gate. Retail success takes time.

New concepts and ideas don't necessarily guarantee success for established retailers, but standing still guarantees failure. That's why winning retailers are constantly in motion, always tweaking their current model, and often experimenting with new concepts, sizes, and applications.

Tomorrow's hot ideas will change the face of retail. Reading consumer trends, leveraging core strengths, finding a defensible market position, and doing all of this profitably are not easy tasks. Yet they're necessary for long-term survival.

New concepts often don't pan out. Winning retailers learn from these efforts, often applying elements of so-called failed concept stores as ways to improve existing stores. The greatest failure among retailers—and the most common trait among stores that wind up in the Black Hole—is failure to innovate.

What does all this mean for a retailer looking to develop a hot idea for tomorrow?

First, retailers should reexamine where hot ideas come from: They are customer-driven (based on consumer trends and demographic changes); they are internally driven (based on a retailer's capabilities); and they are driven (or at least filtered) by competition (avoiding the steamrollers like retail giants Wal-Mart or Home Depot) and by seizing untapped market niches.

Let's do what all great retailers do and begin with the customer. Four national demographic trends, we believe, offer fertile ground for hot ideas: (1) graying baby boomers, (2) maturing Generation Yers, also known as *boomlets,* or the *echo boom,* (3) increasing ethnic diversity, and (4) the haves and have-nots.

## HOME-HAPPY BOOMERS

Where will aging boomers focus their energies, attention, and pocketbooks? That's probably the biggest question facing marketers and retailers today. At 81 million strong, the boomers are the nation's biggest and most affluent consumer group. The stores these consumers opt for will be the envy of the retail industry in coming years.

We know, as we mentioned earlier, that these shoppers are experienced and demanding. Historically, people at this stage in life tend to spend more on travel and less on things like clothing. Hard to say whether boomers will follow that pattern or break the mold, but it seems likely that travel will be a staple of boomer-style retirement.

In general, these customers have moved through the life stages of raising families. They have already taken care of providing for the

**183**

necessities of life. Now, instead of making purchases to meet basic needs, these customers are buying things they've always wanted. They're purchasing more out of desire.

A big trend that has been emerging for years is known as *cocooning,* meaning simply that people are spending more money on their homes. We believe this trend is likely to gain momentum because boomers are viewing their homes as an expression of themselves, as an oasis. It also happens to be, in many cases, their key financial asset. They are looking to upgrade, personalize, and expand their cocoon. They are looking to fill their homes with products they have always wanted rather than those they have needed.

We think two of the most exciting new concepts going after these home-minded consumers are the home-improvement/home-remodeling superstores the Great Indoors, a unit of Sears, and Home Depot's Expo Design Center. Both, by the way, are in an almost life-and-death struggle to master all of the key dynamics of retail success before their parent companies lose patience.

These large stores are designed to solve the needs of consumers who are completing major home remodeling or decorating projects. Each store in its own right offers a "wow" experience, as customers are able to stroll from lavish kitchen setups to bathroom scenes that look as though they've been lifted directly from the pages of *Architectural Digest* or *Better Homes and Gardens*. The stores are staffed with experts who can help people do it themselves or provide a network of contractors to do the work for them.

Home Depot currently has about 50 Expo stores, and Sears has about 20 Great Indoors. Both retailers had announced plans for significant growth only to put new stores on hold while working on the concept's profitability. The biggest difference between the two concepts is that the Great Indoors devotes much more floor space to things like linens, pots and pans, and small appliances. This allows shoppers to complete and accessorize a major project, and it gives the Great Indoors an opportunity to make a sale to customers still planning their dream remodeling project.

These stores are special because they combine all the components needed to complete a major project under one roof. As anyone who's tried to oversee something like a kitchen renovation will tell you, a job like that can involve cabinets, countertops, and electrical work in addition to small and major appliances, flooring, painting, and plumbing. Before the development of these stores, a consumer might have to visit dozens of stores or hire a general contractor to coordinate all these components. The Great Indoors and Expo Design Center offer one-stop shopping for home remodeling jobs. They are true solution sellers (Easy-Est) because of their ability to meet all of the consumer's needs.

No question, Sears and Home Depot have tapped into a powerful consumer trend. They've also done a good job in helping customers understand the benefits of this radical new concept.

The biggest problem with these stores to date has been managing acceptable returns. These big, complex, labor-intensive stores are going after affluent customers who are extremely discerning and have plenty of shopping options. Two similar concepts have already wound up in the Black Hole: House-2-Home (a last-ditch effort of Home Base, a home-improvement store that couldn't escape the steamroller of Home Depot) and Dekor, an overmatched start-up founded by former Home Depot executives.

In a less ambitious, but certainly successful approach, chains like Pottery Barn and Crate & Barrel are doing a masterful job of tapping into increased spending on the home. Retailers should take note that this aging demographic still packs buying power in traditional areas like apparel. While most retailers are obsessed with serving youth (and for good reason), there also remains a huge market for aging boomers. Chico's has been wildly successful in catering to the needs of this older demographic, selling loosely structured, easy-care clothing.

Others would be wise not to ignore the 80 million boomers as they enter a new life stage.

## TWO APPROACHES TO GENERATION Y: GET THE PARENTS, GET THE KIDS

The birth rate explosion after World War II that gave us the first baby boom created a secondary—and almost as sizable—birth boom when baby boomers hit their childbearing years. This generation that's coming of age in the days of the ubiquitous Internet, cell phone connectivity, antiglobalization riots, and fears about homeland security is a customer group of 70 million, ages 6 to 24. Look for smart marketers and retailers to turn their attention in coming years from boomers to Generation Y.

For decades, teens have been important mall customers. As retailers prepare to win over the massive and savvy Generation Y population, we're seeing two trends emerge among retailers: (1) Create stores geared toward younger kids that provide a shopping experience equally enjoyed by kids and their parents. (2) Create stores that appeal directly to teens and older boomlets, where kids are welcomed but their parents aren't.

Two of the best examples of parent-driven Generation Y retailers are Build-A-Bear Workshop and American Girl Place.

Saint Louis–based Build-A-Bear is one of the best-executed retail concepts we've seen in many years. The attention to detail and to the target customer is brilliant. For those unfamiliar with the store, Build-A-Bear allows children to create their own teddy bears. A customer chooses a bearskin from about 20 varieties, then takes it to a filling station and watches it get stuffed. A customer can customize the bear in many ways—from the sounds it will make to its wardrobe and name. Customers can even fill out adoption papers! The experience and the store are thrilling for both children and parents.

In addition to being an astute retailer that manages to smoothly blend creating an experience and selling products, Build-A-Bear incorporates two powerful concepts that are becoming big factors in tomorrow's hot ideas: (1) *narrow generational targeting* (focusing on a very specific audience) and (2) *personalization* (the ability to create a product that can be made to the customer's exact specifications).

The unanswered question for Build-A-Bear concerns staying power. How often, and for how long, will children want to repeat the experience? Many concepts have their best years early on, then fade because they fail to keep the consumer intrigued. We believe Build-A-Bear's management team has the talent to clear this hurdle.

American Girl is a phenomenon that managed to make the leap from being a catalog with a loyal following to opening a retail store that's become a major destination. In the process, American Girl has become a well-known and powerful brand.

American Girl sells historic dolls that come complete with a history book that gives young girls a glimpse of what life was like for girls in an earlier era of American history.

Sensing that it needed to make the store a special destination, American Girl decided to include a theater and restaurant in its store, which is just off Chicago's tony North Michigan Avenue. The restaurant, a popular spot for tourists, includes place settings and special chairs so the dolls can sit at the table. The theater puts on American Girl revues where young performers act out the stories of the American Girl dolls. Like Build-A-Bear, American Girl is a narrowly focused concept that also keeps parents engaged.

The only real problem has been determining how to sustain and capitalize on the store's tremendous success. American Girl, now owned by toy giant Mattel, is grappling with the question of whether to add more stores. While it would certainly increase sales, store expansion could ultimately be detrimental to the mystique of the flagship and its air of exclusivity. In other words, if there were American Girl stores in every mall, would the concept still be so special? Whatever the eventual result, American Girl is a great story that forward-looking retailers should know. A second store has opened on New York's Fifth Avenue. It will undoubtedly engender the same buzz that met store number one. If the stores are kept scarce, the concept should be able to travel selectively.

A new breed of stores, cropping up at malls nationwide, target older Generation Y members, mostly teens, by offering stores and products that come directly from the youth culture. These stores have grown so rapidly that many malls now feature a teen wing, where like stores are grouped together.

Abercrombie & Fitch was the first of this breed, bringing the worn and scruffy look of college undergrads to malls nationwide. Their scandalous magazine featuring scantily clad young adults is precisely the "parent turnoff, kid turn-on" kind of marketing that keeps customers loyal. Abercrombie has spawned a legion of followers, such as American Eagle and Aeropostale, which have both had excellent runs. Wet Seal caters to young women, as does Bebe stores. Journeys is a teen-focused shoe store chain from a surprising parent, Genesco, better known for the enormously staid Johnson & Murphy.

We think one of the best examples is a chain called Hot Topic, which in a way has become the retail embodiment of MTV. Hot Topic says its merchandise "reflects a variety of music related lifestyles, which include street wear, retro influenced lounge, punk, club, and gothic." Hot Topic is everything about the music *except* the music. Hot Topic works because it's authentic (MTV plays at Hot Topic's California headquarters 24/7) and because its employees and management are cued in to the fast-moving fashion whims of its customers. CEO Betsy McLaughlin spends some of her Saturdays working as a salesclerk and makes it a point to read customer comment cards. When asked about the company's impressive string of monthly sales gains (a herculean accomplishment given the fickle fashion sensibilities of its teenage customers), Hot Topic management gives a simple explanation: "We don't try to create trends. We react to trends."

Hot Topic garnered lots of press as one of few retailers that didn't take a big sales hit after the terrorist attacks of September 11, 2001. We learned part of the reason why when we sat on a panel with McLaughlin about a month after the attacks. We were discussing the fact that retailers, in the wake of the postattack drop in consumer spending, would have too much inventory for the upcoming Christmas shopping season. McLaughlin said it wasn't an issue for Hot Topic. The company had not yet ordered its Christmas merchandise—and this was in October.

While Hot Topic's splashy merchandise grabs lots of headlines, what really makes the company so revolutionary is its speed-to-market capabilities. Hot Topic creates and moves product fast. Hot Topic doesn't operate a massive central warehouse facility. Hot Topic doesn't bother with things like vendor rebates or ad planning, so there's no need to order merchandise far in advance. Products pretty much go directly from manufacturer to stores. Within days or just a couple weeks of seeing certain trendsetters like Kid Rock or members of bands like No Doubt or Korn wearing something, Hot Topic can have a version of that style on its sales floors. Many retailers are moving toward faster time to market, but few can keep pace with Hot Topic.

We also think the company may have another winner with a new chain called Torrid, which targets large-size teenage girls. No other store has pursued this vastly underserved customer, and nobody else could do it with the aplomb of Hot Topic. For instance, Torrid sells a T-shirt that reads: "Notice Me: Your Boyfriend's About To."

## INCREASING ETHNIC DIVERSITY

Another big demographic shift that will spark hot ideas in the future is the surge in the nation's ethnic population. By 2010, blacks, Asians, and Hispanics are projected to make up about one-third of the total U.S. population. We are just now beginning to see profound ethnic influences on the foods we eat, the music we listen to, and the clothes we wear.

There's great opportunity for retailers to target these demographic groups—all of which are growing faster than the overall population. But the bigger opportunity is seizing on ethnic-inspired foods, fashions, and lifestyle trends and interpreting them for the general market. Tiger Woods isn't such a hot celebrity endorser just because he's the world's greatest golfer and has a million-dollar smile—although those things certainly help. Tiger's multiethnic heritage personifies our emerging national profile and has helped make him a superstar. The big story and the big opportunity for retailers is to recognize and react to the new multiculturalization of America.

As is true with many trends, music and food often lead the way. Some of today's hottest pop-music stars are Latino: Marc Anthony, Jennifer Lopez, and Ricky Martin. In food, we're seeing a host of restaurants try to develop into the first nationwide purveyors of authentic ethnic food. There are multi-billion-dollar fast-food industries for hamburgers, pizzas, and sub sandwiches. In the future we will no doubt see huge sales volumes for restaurants that sell high-quality Mexican, Asian, and Indian food in fast-food settings. Witness the founders and backers of restaurants such as Pei Wei, Pick up Stix, Baja Fresh, and Chipotle Grill.

One of the most promising entrants in this arena is Chipotle. The restaurant, founded by a classically trained chef, is now owned by McDonald's. It features only fresh ingredients and has a compact menu that focuses on large burritos and a few other Mexican specialties filled with chicken or beef. Chipotle works because of its unique offer, its simple menu, its exciting ambience, and its high-quality food. It also works because it brings more authentic Mexican food to the masses at a time when the masses are just beginning to gain a greater appreciation for ethnic foods.

Chipotle can win with its existing format today, but the bar will be raised in coming years as it faces more competition. McDonald's rival, Wendy's, has purchased a similar concept called Baja Fresh. We think Chipotle will probably have to add more products and diversify its menu once it is no longer the only "quick-casual" Mexican restaurant in town. Essentially, its ability to be Hot-Est will be challenged as competition becomes more intense. The ultimate success of Chipotle depends on what the company does now to prepare for that day.

## HAVES AND HAVE-NOTS

We all know about the stores catering to the haves. Let's face it—the rich are fascinating to most people and garner plenty of ink. The press, in particular, seems to have a fascination with high-end retailing, which is featured prominently in society columns and business sections. While the latest goings-on from Prada, Gucci, and Armani may make for good press, they cater to a minuscule portion of the population. When we're asked to comment on the latest boutique to hit Rodeo Drive in Beverly Hills, Oak Street in Chicago, or Madison Avenue in New York, we are always quick to mention market size. A fabulously successful "have" retailer, Tiffany's, is now a $1.7 billion business. Impressive, yes, but it pales in comparison to the dollars generated by more mundane concepts.

There's long been a bias against establishing retail stores that cater to low-income shoppers. One obvious reason: The founders and backers of retail chains are not low-income people, so they tend to be more interested in the lives of the haves than the have-nots. Another reason: The have-nots have limited spending power.

It's understandable that more retailers don't cater to low-income shoppers. Of course, Wal-Mart has proved that there's tremendous potential here. Yet despite Wal-Mart's amazing success, we think that's just a sliver of the possibilities in targeting America's have-nots.

In addition to discounters like Wal-Mart, Kmart, and Target, another have-not-oriented category has flourished in recent years: dollar stores.

A little-known story of retail in recent years is that by just about every measure—new-store growth, same-store sales increases, profitability, customer shopping frequency—dollar stores are the retail industry's leading performers.

The top three (Dollar General, Family Dollar, and Dollar Tree) added more than 1,600 new stores each year in 2002 and 2003, while same-store monthly sales increased about 6 percent. These three companies also topped blue-chip retailers like Wal-Mart, Costco, and Home Depot at profitability measures such as return on investment (margin times turnover) and return on assets (income divided by assets).

Part of the reason dollar stores remain obscure is because there's confusion and lack of a clear definition of the format. The purest definition is probably the least accurate—stores that sell all merchandise for $1 or less. While such stores exist, the larger and better-known chains have taken a broader view of their assortments and pricing, because the $1 price point is really an artificial barrier.

We prefer a new definition that defines these stores as "convenience discount retailers." This best sums up the philosophy: the marriage of low prices with small, convenient neighborhood locations that offer a limited assortment of general merchandise. These are the modern five-and-dimes. But they've forged a new niche in competing with the discount giants because the convenience discount stores—or dollar stores—are more accessible to people who don't have cars. They also offer convenience for shoppers who can't afford to stock up because they're living from paycheck to paycheck.

In addition to the top three, there are dozens of smaller dollar stores across the country. Consolidation is inevitable, but the opportunities are vast. Nationwide, 55 percent of Americans now shop at a dollar store once a week, up from 47 percent in 1998. This is a category that has been hot for several years and one we believe will continue to be hot well into the future. There are opportunities to expand into urban and suburban markets. Given consumer and economic trends, the need for stores that deliver value will continue.

## LOOKING INSIDE FOR HOT IDEAS

Companies also can look internally to find hot ideas—either by realizing they are neglecting certain customers or by finding ways to leverage existing brands and extend them to new customers.

Such internal analysis often comes in response to competitive activity or from the desire to create new growth vehicles. Regardless, these efforts are most successful when they closely mirror consumer trends and behaviors. The great advantage of brand extension is that new ideas that incorporate the names of well-known retail brands have more credibility with consumers than start-ups with unfamiliar names that have no track record with customers.

The Limited has been the master of creating new formats that extend its brand to meet product demand or demographic opportunity. Bath & Body Works and Victoria's Secret were both Limited spin-offs. The Limited also has segmented its customers with offerings like Express and Limited Too, a successful new format that targets preteens.

In fact, The Limited is so good at this that its spin-offs are now hatching spin-offs. Limited Too recently tried to launch Mish Mash, a new store targeting girls ages 12 to 17. The premise, to give the same girls who were shopping Limited Too a store to graduate to. The problem: That is fairly crowded ground today and is also being pursued by Express (yes, another Limited spin-off). Can the extended brand be extended? Apparently not—Limited is in the process of closing down the chain.

To the credit of Limited, two interesting observations came from Mish Mash. First, it is vital to keep experimenting. The Limited is undaunted in trying new ideas and admitting failure. Second, the company has learned from this effort: The next spin-off from Limited Too is going to be a chain targeting the same demographic but with lower-price-point clothing. (The first store, called Justice, opened in 2004. In retrospect, we think there is a valuable lesson to be learned: It is easier to move *down* in price or in age than up.

The Gap, of course, is no slouch at brand extension. It's had tremendous success with Gap Kids, Gap Baby, and is still spinning its wheels with the new Gap Body, which specializes in underwear. Gap followed demographic shifts when it converted Banana Republic into a fashion-forward store for its older customers and when it created Old Navy to be a discount Gap that also appealed to Gap's younger customers.

Some new and exciting developments in this area include Hot Topic's Torrid, Pottery Barn Kids, and Crate & Barrel's efforts with a funky new store called CB2 and a children's furniture catalog called Land of Nod.

Pottery Barn Kids seems like a surefire winner. Here's a great and established retail brand that's hitting an underserved market: Pottery Barn adult customers who want the same style and quality for their children's furniture. Pottery Barn parent Williams-Sonoma also demonstrated something about the power of multichannel retailing with this concept because it was first launched in early 1999 as a catalog. That allowed Pottery Barn Kids to target existing Pottery Barn customers and gauge demand and tastes through a catalog and web site—without taking on the tremendous costs of opening brick-and-mortar stores. Pottery Barn Teen (son of Mish Mash?) has also been launched as a catalog. The same opportunity could come to retail stores if it meets with success.

Williams-Sonoma is trying this formula again with a home furnishings store called West Elm that features modernistic styles at moderate prices. Launched with great success as a catalog, Williams-Sonoma recently opened its first West Elm store. A relaunched concept called Williams-Sonoma Home is debuting soon as well.

Crate & Barrel, Williams-Sonoma's smaller, privately owned rival, is also trying its hand at brand extension and segmentation. In 2000, Crate opened a small store called CB2 in a gentrified neighborhood on Chicago's North Side. The store features sleek, modern designs in an attempt to reach younger customers. It also features lower prices than Crate & Barrel, which has become increasingly upscale over the years to accommodate aging boomers upgrading their homes. Crate is still toying with the format and merchandise assortments, but should be ready to add a few more stores soon. We think young and young-thinking customers who are looking to spruce up their homes affordably will find CB2 a treat.

For some years, Crate also has considered creating a Crate & Barrel Kids. When a couple of Chicago-area entrepreneurs beat Crate to the punch with a whimsical catalog that featured great-looking kids' furniture and accessories, Crate decided to buy the whole company.

Story has it that Crate founder and CEO Gordon Segal called up this little-known catalog, named Land of Nod after a children's poem, and asked if he could pay them a visit. When he did, Segal gushed that the place reminded him of Crate's early days—the excitement, energy, passion for merchandise, and great visual display. Crate and Land of Nod are now opening Land of Nod stores in the Chicago area. Certainly, Crate will spend a good deal of time experimenting with the Land of Nod store before considering roll-out plans, but any outfit that impresses Segal impresses us. We're looking for exciting things from Land of Nod.

## GO WHERE THE CUSTOMERS ARE

In the movie *Field of Dreams,* the famous line was, "Build it, and they will come." That's long been the modus operandi for retailers:

Build malls or strip centers or stand-alone stores, and the customers will come.

We think it's going to work the opposite way in the future. We'd revise that famous *Field of Dreams* line this way: "Find out where they [your customers] are, and build it there."

Two retail giants are headed that way. Having already converted suburbanites and rural dwellers into customers, Wal-Mart and Home Depot both are experimenting with smaller-format, convenience-oriented stores. These are stores that can be built closer to where customers live.

In the case of Wal-Mart, Neighborhood Market looks suspiciously like a traditional supermarket. While Wal-Mart has been fabulously successful with the supercenter format, these giant stores are the antithesis of Quick-Est and surely are *not* Easy-Est. Neighborhood Market allows the company to penetrate trade areas even further, capturing dollars of customers who simply don't have time to, or don't enjoy shopping in, larger stores. While Wal-Mart is proceeding with caution, look for these stores to be part of its future expansion. We call this concept *market oligopoly,* which enables Wal-Mart to continue to increase its amazing capture of retail dollars.

Lands' End, the Wisconsin-based catalog company known for its affordable, conservative clothes that are a favorite of businesspeople, decided to open its first retail stores (excluding outlet stores) at airports. That's where the company's busy, time-pressed customers are—and where they often spend hours of idle time. In a nod to the increasing informality of the American workplace, Lands' End has also built a burgeoning uniform business, with khakis and denim shirts replacing suits and ties. The Gap's Banana Republic went one step further. As more and more companies ditched their tie-and-jacket dress codes in favor of casual attire, Banana Republic began opening retail stores right in the office buildings of some large companies. These were customers in need, and Banana Republic took the initiative to go to them on the customers' own turf—literally. We don't yet know whether this is a sustainable approach (office politics are always dicey), but we think the lesson is clear. Tomorrow's winning retailers will be the ones that go out of their way to accommodate customers and to meet them at convenient locations.

## WINNING RETAILERS ARE IN MOTION

Competition is unrelenting. Customers are unforgiving. In retail these days, innovation is a necessary tool for survival.

Winning retailers are developing their next concept stores before their core concept hits maturity. While Wal-Mart was rolling out its first-generation discount stores nationwide, the company was developing a new concept in Sam's Club. Then Wal-Mart went to work on a grocery store and discount store combination it called Wal-Mart Supercenters. Today, supercenters are Wal-Mart's main growth engine. That concept is far from maturity at this point, with probably 5 to 10 years of explosive growth ahead, and today Wal-Mart is expanding overseas and fine-tuning its next concept: Neighborhood Markets.

As hard as it is to imagine, if Wal-Mart had been content to stick with the big win of its first-generation Wal-Mart stores, the company would be in decline today. Instead, it's the world's largest retailer and still has bright growth prospects. Too many retailers wait until their current concept is mature before they start searching for a new thing. By contrast, winning retailers like Wal-Mart strive to stay a step ahead. Wal-Mart's next hot idea is well tested and ready for rollout by the time its current formats reach maturity. Wal-Mart is a master at riding the S curve, hitting upon innovation and growth before concepts begin to decline. Sears didn't do that. Toys "R" Us didn't do that. Montgomery Ward didn't do that.

# WINNING AT RETAIL

Remember, while new concepts and ideas don't guarantee success, standing still guarantees failure. Winning retailers are in motion. Experimentation is critical to keep pace with fast-changing consumer attitudes and behaviors. Tomorrow's hot ideas are out there for retailers willing to innovate and experiment at trying to solve customers' problems.

## CHAPTER ELEVEN

# PUTTING THE CUSTOMER IN CONTROL

Est explains why retailers win or lose. They must own a definitive attribute in the customer's mind. In today's highly competitive business environment, they must respond to consumer trends if they hope to unlock tomorrow's hot new ideas. The common thread throughout *Winning at Retail* is that the customer must be at the center of a retailer's thinking. Know and respond properly to the customer, and a retailer can achieve astounding results, no matter if the playing field is crowded.

If the customer is really the common denominator, is there one direction in the future that would benefit all retailers, no matter which Est position they choose? We believe there is. We call it *putting the customer in control*.

Retail customers today are shopping for something that too few retailers offer—*efficiency*. Customers want products, store layouts, solutions, and services that maximize the efficiency of their shopping trips. Today's customers are pursuing efficiency with the same zeal that corporate executives look to squeeze out profits. Customers are rewarding stores that offer them efficiency and abandoning stores that are too much work, that don't live up to their promises, or that have offerings that are too limited.

Putting the customer in control is one of retail's next great frontiers. Discount stores like Wal-Mart, warehouse clubs like Costco, and discount convenience stores like Dollar General have driven the price-war game about as far as it can go. Internet retailers like Amazon and eBay offer a vast selection of products that no brick-and-mortar store can match. In other words, the Internet has seemingly taken the Big-Est proposition to the extreme.

That leaves one key differentiator for retailers: enhancing and optimizing the customer experience.

We try to avoid talking too much about creating a wonderful "customer experience." What rang a bell with us once was when a consumer told us in a focus group that an experience is "what you get when you don't get what you expect." Too many retailers associate customer experience with things that make shopping fun and entertaining, or things that try to set moods for customers. While that stuff is fine—some of it is very important—we think it's more critical for retailers to create experiences that are mostly forgettable. Things are forgettable when they go smoothly. We're talking about the kind of shopping trips that are so uneventful and so easy that the customer hardly does any thinking at all. Experiences, on the other hand, tend to happen when things go wrong. Instead of talking about customer experience, we talk about allowing the customer to be in control of the shopping experience. In many ways, this is as radical a concept as any proposed in this book.

When "retail-tainment" was the rage in the early to mid-1990s, we were skeptical. While shopping should be fun and enjoyable, people go to stores to buy things. They may appreciate some bells and whistles along the way, but that's not why they go to a store—and it is hardly ever why they come back.

## Putting the Customer in Control

Thinking about placing the customer in control conveys the message that retailers need to focus on improving the shopping experience in a way that saves customers time, effort, and aggravation. Today's time-starved customers, faced with more shopping choices than ever, are choosing to shop at places that work for them, that are efficient for them.

The notion of putting the customer in control is not yet part of the retail vernacular. How do you achieve it? How do you measure it? These are not simple questions to answer. In this chapter, we discuss how retailers can begin to address this issue.

We also extol the virtues of the "Five Cs of Customer in Control." We highlight stores that succeed and stores that fail at this, and we look at some specific remedies.

To begin, let's talk about something we call the "Tick-Off Factors." Break these four tenets and you'll have unhappy customers wishing they could find a more efficient place to shop:

1. Don't have an item that customers expect to find at your store, or don't have that item in stock or available within the time frame they expect.
2. Make it difficult for customers to find what they are looking for.
3. Don't help the customer figure out what to buy.
4. Employ salespeople who are not helpful or courteous.

You may have noticed that the Tick-Off Factors are the reverse of the customers' definition of great customer service. Customers want products to be in stock; they want stores to be logically laid out so they don't waste time; they want information readily available to help them make a decision; and they want to deal with knowledgeable, friendly salespeople. Eliminate the Tick-Off Factors, and your stores will simultaneously provide better service and be more efficient for customers.

## RETAILER EFFICIENCY VERSUS CUSTOMER EFFICIENCY

Retailers have always focused on efficiency—their own. By and large, they were able to get away with focusing on their own needs. Almost by default, they were often the only game in town. Besides, most stores behaved in exactly the same manner. However, in the past 10 to 20 years, as the industry has gotten increasingly competitive, retailers have stepped up their efforts to drive down operating costs while increasing sales productivity. Some of these efforts to improve efficiency have been good for customers (faster and more accurate scanners and computers, high-speed connectivity, more efficient and faster materials handling and distribution capabilities, more accurate inventory and reporting systems, etc.), but too often, these so-called efficiency efforts run counter to the customer's efficiency.

For example, if a retailer reduces the number of salesclerks on its floors, customers must work harder at finding and deciding what to buy. If a retailer requires checkout clerks to answer telephones, customers must wait longer to be helped. If a retailer crams its aisles with products stacked atop pallets or deploys long gondola runs to increase actual selling space, customers must work harder to navigate the store.

In theory, all these things improve the retailer's productivity: Fewer clerks mean lower costs; multitasking checkout clerks who answer telephones save money; more products in the aisles increase sales opportunities. In reality, the retailer is wasting customers' time with these strategies, and thereby makes their shopping trip less efficient.

This reinforces one of the unpleasant truths of this business: Most retailers do not really put customers first. On a lighter note, it reminds us of the hilarious TV show *Fawlty Towers,* where John

# Putting the Customer in Control

Cleese plays a frustrated innkeeper. In one classic scene, Cleese is at the check-in desk, working on paperwork and handling phone calls. He looks up and notices a long line of agitated customers. Exasperated, Cleese berates his customers: "All you people ever do is gripe, gripe, gripe! You pounce in here, expecting to be waited on hand and foot. Can't you see I've got a business to run here? Have you any idea how much there is to do? Do you ever think of that? Of course not!"

Too many retailers are guilty of making their employees feel like that. Sales associates who are given the task of restocking the sales floor in between waiting on customers know that they're judged by progress. Their success will be measured by how well they have restocked the store. What's not measured: Did they ignore customers while busily restocking? When asked for help, did they give terse answers or vague directions and hustle back to restocking—the task that essentially measures their performance?

Retailers meticulously measure their own productivity as well as the productivity of employees. Retailers want their assets—people, real estate, inventory—to be as productive as possible in terms of sales per worker-hour, sales per square foot, and inventory turns. As an equation, productivity equals sales divided by assets. With the success of Wal-Mart and other discount-oriented retailers over the past couple decades, much of the retailer productivity focus has been on decreasing the denominator (assets) as a way to increase productivity. That's a short-term fix. The real long-term strategy is to try to work on the numerator (sales), not just by adding new stores, but by making things great for customers so they buy more and recruit other customers.

That's a tough order, and the immediate profit boost isn't there, so many retailers insist on attacking the denominator. Armed with a mission to reduce operating and merchandising costs, retailers have depleted their inventories, cut payroll hours, eliminated phone lines and added voice-mail systems (have you ever been lost in voice mail hell?), cut back on signage and point-of-sale information, and decreased aisle space to make way for more merchandise displays.

The end result: Many stores have pushed the equation too far. They've created stores that focus too much on maximizing the retailer's productivity. In turn, many of these stores become too inefficient for customers. A recent study found that 64 percent of consumers say they will leave a store if checkout takes too long, and 70 percent say they make a point to shop at stores that don't waste their time.

Still, some retailers don't pay any heed to customer efficiency. Either they don't think it's important, or they don't understand how to measure and improve it. These retailers need to wake up soon, because customer efficiency will be a key element of future success in retailing.

## THE FIVE CS OF PUTTING THE CUSTOMER IN CONTROL

Historically, much of retailing has been about selling products that the retailer wants the customers to buy. The retailer pushes certain products, either because those products have fat profit margins or because the retailer has too many of those products and needs to sell them quickly to optimize the value of the inventory. Those motivations will probably never go away. But increasingly, retailers that focus on improving the shopping experience—particularly in ways that make shopping more productive—will win. They will continue to take customers away from stores that insist on focusing on their own problems rather than customers' problems. There are five fundamental elements to creating an efficient shopping experience. We call them the Five Cs of Customer in Control: (1) concept clarity, (2) choice clarity, (3) control of the experience, (4) communications of the concept, (5) closure. (See Figure 11.1.)

**FIGURE 11.1** Five Cs of Customer in Control

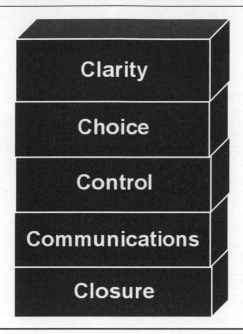

*Clarity*

Customers want to know what retailers offer and what they stand for. Stores must be crystal clear about what products and services they offer and what their basic value proposition is to customers. Stores that don't have clearly defined positionings confuse customers, and as a result their customers will go elsewhere—probably to a store with better clarity, where customers know exactly what they're getting.

The key to clarity is segmentation. Stores must set themselves off as distinct by being focused on certain products, certain customers, or a certain Est proposition.

Category killers have product clarity. Toys "R" Us is all about toys. Golfsmith is all about golf merchandise and apparel. Home Depot is all about home-improvement products. Container Store is a phenomenal example of product clarity and integrity. It sells nothing but organizational products. The company could probably add some sales by adding a few nonrelated products here and there, but it accepts an intelligent loss of sales in order to maintain its great clarity.

One of the great benefits of clarity, and it certainly bolsters the Container Store's business, is that clarity increases store productivity. Why? Customers at the Container Store know exactly what the store is about. They are there because they have an organizational problem to be solved. In turn, these are active customers who are ready and willing to spend.

Stores like REI and Eastern Mountain Sports appeal to customers who live a certain lifestyle—namely, they enjoy outdoor sports like camping, hiking, mountain climbing, and kayaking. Whole Foods is another example of clarity through customer segmentation. It's designed to serve customers who want organic and gourmet foods. Pier One targets people who want to decorate their homes with reasonably priced, eclectic decor. Hot Topic is all about the MTV audience.

The strength of these concepts is human nature: Birds of a feather flock together. Stores that do a good job of achieving clarity through customer segmentation are sure to be aided by lots of word of mouth.

Clarity can also come from Est positioning. Wal-Mart is Cheap-Est. Fast-food chains like McDonald's and Wendy's are Quick-Est. These are crystal clear value propositions for customers.

The way that retailers establish and enhance clarity is to execute clearly and consistently. They also must have consistent messages between their marketing and their store operations. Consistency breeds clarity. Inconsistency breeds confusion. We have toyed with the notion of making *consistency* our sixth *C*. Certainly, great retailers execute over and over again.

A once-great retailer that has struggled for more than a decade without clarity is Sears. The retailer doesn't have clarity among its products or customers. It does not have an Est position. While Sears has stopped and started with numerous retail turnarounds over the years, the company must establish some clarity of purpose before its stores will thrive once again.

## Choice

Too much choice or too little choice is a customer disservice—it wastes time, and it can actually make customers less likely to make a purchase. Customers want retailers to be their buying agents. They want the selection already edited to be exactly right for them, so they have to make a few well-defined decisions based on just the right amount of choice.

Two professors, one from Columbia University and one from Stanford University, published a paper in the December 2000 issue of the *Journal of Personality and Social Psychology* that illustrated the perils of too much choice.

In one study, they set up a sample booth for jams at an upscale grocery store. At times the booth featured six types of jam; at other times it featured 24 different jams. The study found that while the larger assortment attracted more shoppers, far fewer of those shoppers actually made a purchase. Of the people who stopped to sample from the six jams, 30 percent bought a jar of jam. Of the shoppers who stopped to sample when presented with 24 different jams, only 3 percent made a purchase.

In another study, subjects were asked to choose one of six flavors of Godiva chocolate to eat. Another group of subjects was asked to choose among 30 flavors. The subjects presented with six options were more satisfied with their choice. The subjects given 30 options found the chocolates they had selected less enjoyable. They were even less likely to accept chocolates as compensation for taking part in the study!

The presentation of overwhelming choice made them too uncertain and, ultimately, dissatisfied with their decision. A good retailer tries not to let that happen, because it's bad for customers and it's bad for business.

When we study stores for *Retail Watch* articles, we usually bring along a small camera and snap a few pictures. Some of them make it into our slide presentations. Here are two of our favorites:

The first slide shows a 40-foot aisle from the now-defunct Phar-Mor discount drugstore with the store's toothpaste assortment. Just toothpaste—40 feet of it—seemingly every brand, subbrand, taste, size, and color. Who, other than an obsessed dental hygienist, would want to spend that much time selecting a tube of toothpaste?

The next slide shows an aisle that had to be more than 50 feet long from French retail giant Carrefour, snapped at one of its failed attempts at establishing a hypermarket in the United States. The massive aisle featured one brand of laundry detergent. One brand. Give shoppers at least a cheap selection and a premium selection. (Every shopper in the store had to walk past those 50 feet to get to the next item or product category.) Too little choice was one reason the hypermarkets failed to excite American consumers.

Of course, these are extremes. But finding that right amount of choice is a key factor for retailers. We think it's one of the reasons Kohl's is clobbering department stores right now. Kohl's provides customers a few choices of an apparel style, organized together based on colors, brands, and prices. Kohl's offers an adequate choice and helps customers manage that choice through its good organization. Department stores scatter a far larger selection—probably too large—and organize it in a way that makes sense only to the department stores and the fashion houses who sell to them.

# Putting the Customer in Control

## *Control*

Customers today want to be in control. This is the central premise of this chapter. Thanks to a decades-long shift toward self-service—from pumping gas to paying for groceries—customers are willing and actually even prefer to help themselves. They will buy from retailers that respect their time and intelligence and that help make their shopping experience more productive.

Because much of retail's history has been about selling products the retailer wants to sell (those with high margins and overstocks), retailers have long attempted to control customers. That's why retailers so often bury top-selling products in the back of the store. That's why supermarkets and stores like Toys "R" Us used to have layouts that forced shoppers to walk past all merchandise. That's why drugstores have high-margin cosmetics near their entrances and their pharmacies in the corner farthest from the front door.

It's more than store layout, though. Supermarkets are grabbing for control with their loyalty-card programs. By featuring certain brands at huge discounts—often after making all the brands considerably more expensive than previously—they're forcing customers to buy that discounted brand or feel like idiots. In essence, the grocery stores and vendors they partner with are forcing customers to buy what they want to sell. Auto dealers try to put their salespeople in control, too: They know the fair value of the car, while the customer must try to haggle from the so-called sticker price.

CarMax is a company that turned the game upside down and put customers in control by giving them one honest price, by sharing a used car's history with customers, and by providing a standard quality test. Walgreens' put customers in control when it offered them drive-through pharmacy windows.

Retailers need to give customers control by making their stores easier to shop and by providing key information. Giving customers control empowers them and makes them come to see a retailer as an advocate rather than an adversary. In many situations, when retailers let the customer "do it themselves," they indirectly save on payroll expense as well.

Maybe the most revolutionary aspect of the Internet and e-commerce is the power it has given consumers: to shop when they want to shop, where they want to shop, with huge amounts of information available about what they're buying. Many sites even give customers the choice of how much to pay for the products they are interested in. Customers have more control than ever before.

Other new technologies are also allowing customers to take control. ATMs were the pioneers in this area, but more and more we are seeing self-scanners and even in-aisle scanners in retail stores, both of which allow customers to control the checkout process. In fact, it is estimated that more than 13,000 self-checkout scanners will be in place in U.S. retail stores by early 2004. Home Depot alone estimates that more than 100 million self-checkout transactions occurred in its stores during the first week of December 2003. Customers have clearly accepted being in control.

### Communications

Today's efficiency-minded customers are hungry for information. They want help to find what they're looking for, and they want the information that leads them to that product to be consistent and efficient—whether it comes from signs, salespeople, the phone, or the Internet. Once customers have found what they're looking for, they want help making their purchasing decision.

Deciding what information to provide customers and when, how, and where to provide it are critically important to improving customer efficiency. Even our cheapest retailer, Wal-Mart, is installing new signage in its supercenters: navigational signs in main aisles to help customers locate various departments and smaller departmental signs to help customers locate specific categories. Signage unrelated to these two objectives, which was clearly visible in the past, is no longer allowed. The result: a cleaner overall look, less signage expenses, and improved shopping efficiency for customers.

Directional and destinational signs are critical elements of customer communications. They need to be simple and they need to be visible. Stores that excel in communications, like Target and CVS, use color coding and different floor surfaces to set off different parts of the store. Customers pick up on these cues, and it makes it easier for them to find their way. A number of years ago, we worked with one of our Quick-Est retailers, McDonald's, to develop a new communication and signing system at the drive-through windows. Using presale message boards, menus that rotate according to time of day, and electronic confirmation windows (for improving order accuracy), McDonald's significantly improved the customer efficiency of its drive-through operations (which, by the way, contribute to almost 60 percent of McDonald's total restaurant sales).

Today, most retailers tend to err on the side of too little communication, but we have also seen the opposite: communication overload, or *clutter*. This typically happens when different parts of the retail organization (and its associated vendors) all want to have their message in front of the customer. Without a central organization to manage and control communications (we call them *clutter busters*), unimportant messages normally overwhelm the critical ones. A magic number for retailing communications is three . . . three messages. If a retailer tries to communicate more than three messages at a single customer touch point, the customer often tunes out.

Communication involves displaying prices in an obvious way and organizing comparable, yet distinct, products near one another in a way that helps explain the differences between them. For complex, big-ticket purchases, good retailers are using the Internet as a communication tool to help customers research and better understand their options. It's always been important for retailers to be consistent across communication channels—from store to phone to catalog. The emergence of the Internet, along with customers' increasing desire to be in control and shop how and when they like, makes it more vital than ever for retailers to keep their messages consistent across channels.

### *Closure*

Nothing is a more blatant waste of customers' time—real or perceived—than inefficient handling of a shopping trip's conclusion. According to Tom Heymann (*On an Average Day*), Americans spend more than 100 million hours a day waiting in line. You can count on it that they don't enjoy the wait. Customers today demand efficient and competent closure, whether related to checkout, pickup, delivery, or returns.

Retailers have been shooting themselves in the foot for decades by mishandling checkout. In some ways, the importance of providing a quick, efficient checkout is an issue of perception. Checkout is the last thing customers do when they shop at a store, so it tends to be the most memorable part of the shopping trip—particularly when it's handled poorly. The biggest problems are inadequate staffing and lousy handling of "exceptions" (the customer who has an unusual problem and requires a lot of time to service).

Customers don't mind waiting in line for a few minutes when they can see that every checkout register is in use. But they don't like to wait behind three or four people in one line when they see that half the registers are closed.

In recent years, retailers have made some progress. More stores have adopted express aisles for customers with small purchases. Kroger and many other supermarkets have implemented self-checkout where customers scan their own goods and handle their own checkout. Whether this truly saves customers time or not, there's a *perception* that it does. Additionally, this lets shoppers be in control. This practice is now being adopted by retailers like Home

Depot and Wal-Mart. It has tremendous benefits to retailers in saving on labor costs, and it also empowers the consumer.

Department stores often fail at checkout because of their decentralized layout and multiple checkout booths. These are often too hard for customers to find and too hard for store managers to keep staffed, as it's impossible to predict when each checkout area will be swamped or empty. (Separate departments can fluctuate dramatically and unpredictably.) That's why stores like Sears and J.C. Penney are beginning to convert to the central checkout method employed by supermarkets and discount stores.

Retailers must adopt policies to move all exceptions away from their checkout areas to a designated customer service window and/or use snaking-type waiting lines such as you see at airports, Best Buy, Fry's, Borders, and other high-volume retailers. This way, customers with special problems will not feel as though they are seriously delaying others behind them in line. It also helps the customers waiting in line to feel as though the store is doing everything it can to serve them as quickly and fairly as possible.

Closure also includes pickup, delivery, and returns. As with exceptions, these things should be handled in separate, clearly marked areas. The key to handling these efficiently is to keep customers informed.

One great example is a new system developed by Sears to improve its pickup process. In the past, if you bought a large item like a big-screen TV or a treadmill, you had to first pay for it. Then you got a receipt to take to the pickup area. There you invariably found a long line where you waited your turn to hand over that receipt, then had to wait once again while employees found your item. Sears figured out a way to mechanize this process and cut out several steps and the amount of time waiting idly in line. Instead of the pickup window, there's a computer monitor where you enter your order number. The computer verifies the order, tells you where the product is, and tells you how many minutes you'll have to wait before the product shows up.

The process may still take as long as it did before, although our personal experience is that it's markedly faster, but by giving customers more information, the wait is infinitely more tolerable. Closure is the final moment of truth for customers, and it's one they don't soon forget. Stores must improve closure to satisfy customers who are shopping for efficiency.

## CUSTOMERS IN CONTROL: GUIDELINES TO LIVE BY

Understanding the Five Cs and how they relate to an individual retailer is the first step in improving customer efficiency. The next step is to try to gauge areas that are inefficient for customers and correct the problems there. In other words, remove the roadblocks to customer efficiency by focusing on each step of the customer experience . . . one step at a time.

The critical caveat here is that retailers must initially focus solely on the customer experience. They should disregard concerns about productivity, or why it would be too expensive, or why they don't have the money, the floor space, the people, or the technology to solve the problem. Retailers must start by forgetting about their own interest and focusing only on the customer's interest. Otherwise, most of the best fixes are likely to be shot down.

Remember, put customers first. Start by thinking only about customer efficiency, and set out to create the perfect world for customers. Retailers may not be able to execute that perfect world—and they may not want to for economic reasons. But it's a starting point from whence a retailer can determine what it *can* do and also look for the least costly ways to execute the changes needed to improve customer efficiency.

## Putting the Customer in Control

The best way to find roadblocks is to study customers shopping in your stores. Another way is for retail executives to shop in the stores themselves—and to shop other stores. We know that too few retail executives actually spend much time shopping in stores, experiencing the frustrations and overcoming the obstacles that shoppers must face. One of the primary things we do in our practice is spend time in stores. We watch how customers behave, and we ourselves shop. There's no substitute for that kind of retail intelligence.

Determine the 10 key touch points for customers as they shop. Then, when observing customers, look for areas where shoppers spend an inordinate amount of time. Look for times when they leave an area without buying anything. Look for times when they must be helped by more than one associate. Look for times when customers are making unnecessary or repetitive steps. These are bottlenecks and barriers that a retailer should eliminate to improve customer efficiency.

An effective way to address these customer inefficiencies is through a "zone-fix" approach. Such an approach focuses on a single zone, or touch point, of the customer's shopping experience, and it normally works best when a team is assembled and assigned to improve efficiency in a zone that's problematic for customers. We believe that's what Sears did with its innovative new pickup system. We know that's what car rental companies did some years ago when they developed systems that allowed customers to skip waiting in a line to pick up the keys for their cars. These fixes eliminated unnecessary steps and bottlenecks where customers were frustrated with long waits.

This zone-focus approach is effective because it makes customer efficiency seem more manageable. It also makes it easier for retailers to understand how getting just the right communication and technology delivered to customers at just the right time can improve customer efficiency and increase customer satisfaction.

We've developed a checklist of 10 tactical measures that can improve customer efficiency:

1. Be open days and times when your customers want to shop.
2. Be in stock every day, especially on important, high-volume items.
3. Provide plenty of self-help information for customers.
4. Make sure prices on all items and services are clear and current.
5. Keep checkout times to less than two minutes.
6. Handle exceptions away from the normal checkout areas (or use single snaking-type lines to minimize the inequities in customer waiting).
7. Review and simplify phone-handling processes, procedures, and systems (check out your own voice-mail system once in a while!).
8. Develop consistency in customer policies and handling processes across channels.
9. Ensure that employees are well-trained on products and processes.
10. Review your equipment and computer systems. Make sure they are current, operative, easy to use, and informative.

---

## Five Cs: Kohl's

We think one company that has set the bar for putting the customer in control is Kohl's. We've been big fans for a decade now. We must confess, though, that while we saw the power and potential of Kohl's customer proposition, we didn't know the company would blossom into one of the great retail success stories of the 1990s.

For the uninitiated, Kohl's is a family-oriented, moderately priced, junior department store that sells apparel and home decor. One of our favorite things about Kohl's is that so

---

# Putting the Customer in Control

many Wall Street analysts and big-city business reporters whom we talk to say that they "don't get" Kohl's. We think that's great, because it's a testament to Kohl's razor-sharp focus on its core customers—which are not affluent city dwellers. Kohl's customers are middle-income suburban families looking to buy low-priced, basic fashions from familiar labels, and its customers "get" Kohl's in a big way.

In the late 1990s and early 2000s, Kohl's was one of the nation's fastest-growing and most profitable retail chains. From 1993 through 2002, Kohl's sales grew to $9.1 billion from $1.3 billion. Meanwhile, its earnings increased more than tenfold, to $643 million in 2002 from $54 million in 1993. (See Table 11.1.) As Kohl's pushed into new markets from the late 1990s through 2001, customers lined up hours before new openings to shop at Kohl's. Sure, customers were there for the bargains—Kohl's is extremely promotional—but they also were there to experience Kohl's.

This is a store that understands and respects the needs and desires of its customers—middle-income families on tight budgets. That's a huge sweet spot in the market (in fact, it's the largest portion of the market), and other retailers are scrambling to reach this demographic. It's the market that

**TABLE 11.1**   Performance of Kohl's: A Five Cs Retailer

|  | 1993 | 2002 | Compound Annual Growth Rate (%), 1993–2002 |
|---|---|---|---|
| Net sales ($ millions) | $1306 | $9,120 | 24 |
| Net income ($ millions) | $54 | $643 | 32 |
| Operating profit (%) | 7.8 | 12 | N/A |
| Number of stores | 90 | 457 | 19.6 |

was lost by stores like Montgomery Ward, J.C. Penney, and Sears. These are shoppers looking to find items that are better quality than those available at discount stores, but at lower prices than at most department and specialty stores.

Kohl's appeal goes beyond its product assortment. Other stores, from discount stores to department stores, have similar merchandise. But nobody provides a more efficient shopping experience than Kohl's.

Here is how we rate Kohl's on the Five Cs.

## Clarity

As a family-oriented, moderately priced department store, Kohl's is extremely focused in the categories it carries and in the range of brands and prices within those categories. Everything in its assortment is focused on serving middle-income families on a budget. Kohl's consistently delivers this clarity throughout its stores and in its marketing. It doesn't try to be everything to everybody. Price points are matched to the target audience. Kohl's customers get it instantly. They understand what Kohl's is all about and that it's a store for them. Kohl's does an excellent job of maintaining a clear focus on what it offers and stands for—and communicates that day in and day out through consistent execution.

## Choice

Kohl's limits its choices to well-known major brands and a handful of private labels. The selection runs a relatively narrow range of prices, starting at the high end of discount stores and topping out at the middle range of department stores. Kohl's edits its assortment by brand, size, style, and color to ensure that customers have enough to choose from, yet not so much that they are overwhelmed. Carrying the right amount of products is an enormous benefit to customers. It provides choice without confusion. Remember, both too much and too little choice wastes customers' time. Kohl's also does a better job than most stores at staying in stock on key items. Although maintaining a large inventory increases the risk that merchandise won't sell quickly enough, it is a critical component of being an efficient shopping destination.

### Control

Kohl's puts customers in control by the way it has engineered its stores and the shopping experience, from parking lot to checkout. This is perhaps the most overlooked aspect of Kohl's success. Control begins before the shopper even sets foot in Kohl's. The company tries to avoid locating in malls. Kohl's wants to be in suburban strip centers, where it can have its own parking lot and one entrance. To customers, that makes Kohl's easier to access, especially compared with the massive parking lots and multiple entrances at malls.

Also, Kohl's stores are only about half the size of traditional department stores, and nearly all of them are one-level stores. They're also less daunting than department stores because of Kohl's racetrack-type store layout, which allows shoppers to easily circulate through the entire store. A *Wall Street Journal* article described the racetrack's purpose thus: "to smoothly lead shoppers past all the merchandise, in what the retailer hopes is a continuous circuit of temptation." Kohl's limits the number of display racks near the racetrack. The idea is to avoid clutter, which makes shoppers more willing to leave the racetrack to check out merchandise. Spacing between displays is navigable for Kohl's shopping carts and strollers. For customers, a smaller store that's easy to navigate is more manageable and increases their sense of being in control.

The store layout and design also feature open sight lines, which means people can scan the entire store and easily spot what they're looking for. Although many stores have introduced self-help features, Kohl's actually makes self-help a benefit to customers. For instance, shoes are kept on racks where customers can help themselves; they needn't wait to find a sales clerk who then searches a back room. Help is available at Kohl's, but it's rarely needed because customers are in control and their choices are clear.

Kohl's carries brands that middle-income America knows and trusts. The advantage is threefold. First, Kohl's makes the brands easy to find. Second, Kohl's establishes itself as the go-to source for sought-after brands. Third, and perhaps most important, Kohl's offers brands that are known for quality and value, which gives customers control—because they don't have to worry about whether the quality is good enough.

## Communications

Kohl's communicates its customer proposition as well as any retailer we can think of. Its messages: We have great prices; we are always on sale; we have great brands. The signage system is simple and clear. Departments, categories, and changing rooms are clearly marked, and their presentation, which uses a combination of open sight lines and merchandise tiering, allows customers to easily see and find product categories and items.

Kohl's clearly has thought through its messaging programs. Each customer touch-point zone provides an appropriate balancing of messages, no overload, and typically two to three messages per touch point. Most of Kohl's point-of-sale information is focused in areas like home decor and appliances, where product information is critical to the consumer decision.

# Putting the Customer in Control

From its TV ads to newspaper inserts to in-store signs, Kohl's is crisp and consistent in letting customers know they are saving money when they shop at Kohl's.

## *Closure*

Kohl's is superb at closure—a key area for customer efficiency because customers put so much importance on their experience at checkout. Kohl's operates centralized checkout areas that are staffed full-time, more like those in discount stores and supermarkets than in department stores. Managers ensure that registers are fully staffed when customers are waiting in line. This makes the checkout area easier to find and the checkout process quicker. It also makes it easier for Kohl's to staff appropriately and keep wait times low. Exchange and return policies are well communicated and handled efficiently in a separate area that is clearly visible and easy to find.

Like any retailer, Kohl's is constantly on the firing line to produce continued results. After nearly a decade-long run of exceptional sales and profit gains, Kohl's experienced a tough 2003. The company is still growing at an eye-popping rate, but its comparable store sales are starting to slow. Analysts will come up with all sorts of explanations about why this is occurring. Our take: When we walk into Kohl's stores of late, they are no longer as crisply executing Easy-Est and are beginning to violate the sanctity of putting customers in control. What do we mean? Visits made earlier in 2003 revealed the once-clear central aisles to be cluttered with displays. The stores had too much inventory in their departments, which made them look more like cramped department stores than a pleasing alternative. Predictably, these signs appeared well before their key performance indicators (e.g., comparable store sales) began to slip. Can the company right the ship? Certainly, but the warning signs of potentially losing its Est loom large.

Retailing, after all, is unforgiving, with performance being measured daily. Ultimately, it comes down to execution, day by day, customer by customer. While many retailers continue to excel, it isn't easy being Est—or staying there.

# CHAPTER TWELVE

# A GLANCE
# AT THE FUTURE

*"The future is already here.*
*It's just unevenly distributed."*

—WILLIAM GIBSON

We usually end our formal presentations with this quote by British science fiction writer William Gibson. It is our belief that it is difficult, if not impossible, to develop any plausible predictions about the future more than about five years out. Nowhere is this truer than in the retail business, where changes in the weather, the economy, or fashion can quickly alter short-term results and thus change your long-term trajectory. Norm McMillan, our founder, is always fond of saying that retailers are constantly looking one month into the past and about 15 seconds into the future. This is partly true: We don't know any retail group that isn't fixated on yesterday's sales numbers.

That being said, we firmly believe that there is a way to understand the future if retailers and service companies pay close attention to the trends that are happening around them. This means watching

227

consumers, new competitors, and trends that may be occurring around the world. In our presentations of key trends, we always stress that there isn't just one retailer or format with lessons to learn from, it's a combination of them all. The future is indeed predictable; it just is never neatly packaged. That's why we pay fanatical attention to consumer trends and new retail concepts from around the world, searching for those insights that can predict where business is headed.

One of our clients once assessed McMillan|Doolittle by saying we're good at "stretching the practical." We take this as a great compliment. It means we're looking to the future, but also want to remain grounded in real consumer needs and wants, in addition to the practical financial needs that drive success. Far too often, concepts aimed at the future ignore one or both of these critical components. It has been our experience that labeling anything "store of the future" becomes a code for something that will never make any money.

## FUTURE TRENDS

Here is an intrepid look at the top six trends that will definitively play a huge role in the future of retailing in the course of the next 5 to 10 years:

### The Wal-Mart Factor

The influence of Wal-Mart is like nothing retailing has ever seen. Its sheer size, magnitude, and momentum practically ensures that Wal-Mart, and all things related to Wal-Mart, will dominate retail headlines over the next decade. (See Table 12.1.)

At almost $250 billion in sales in 2002, the company is four times as large as its nearest competitor. More impressively, it shows absolutely no signs of slowing down. It continues to drive both impressive same-store sales as well as rolling out stores at a prodigious pace. Developing Wal-Mart factoids has become its own cottage industry. For example, Wal-Mart controls nearly 10 cents of

# A Glance at the Future

**TABLE 12.1**   Performance of Wal-Mart: The Influencer

|  | 1993 | 2002 | Increase (%), 1993–2002 |
|---|---|---|---|
| Net sales ($ millions) | $55,484 | $244,524 | 16 |
| Net income ($ millions) | $1,995 | $8,039 | 17 |
| Operating profit (%) | 5.4 | 4.8 | N/A |
| Number of stores | 2,136 | 4,688 | 9 |

every retail dollar spent in America, and it controls more than one-third of all diapers purchased. Wal-Mart's annual growth alone would place it among the 10 largest retailers in the United States. Wal-Mart's planned capital expenditures on a year-to-year basis also exceed the next 10 largest companies. And on and on.

Can Wal-Mart continue to grow? Here's what we do know. The company has a relatively clear path in front of it to triple its number of supercenters, opening over 200 locations a year over the next five years. This growth alone provides a compelling story. Wal-Mart has barely scratched the surface of international opportunity. While the road to growth internationally will not be as smooth as in the United States due to cultural barriers, real estate constraints, and significant regulatory hurdles, the company has already had some major successes in countries like Canada, Mexico, and the United Kingdom. We would expect to see acquisition, never a big part of U.S. growth, become a more significant strategy abroad.

New concepts like Neighborhood Market remain in the incubator stage, but the company has proven adept at having a concept ready to roll out just as growth starts to slow. While Neighborhood Market is not proven, we believe the concept has made significant strides and will be ready when needed (when supercenter growth starts to slow).

In the future, we believe that no retail industry is safe from Wal-Mart's reach. It has experimented with furniture retailing, book retailing, and craft retailing, to name a few. It recently shut down a test selling used cars, but we believe it will continue to be intrigued by such a massive business. In sector after sector—from groceries to sporting goods to jewelry to gasoline—Wal-Mart's reach and influence is being profoundly felt.

What stands in its way? We believe that its Est proposition to the consumer—both in the United States and abroad—remains particularly compelling. Wal-Mart simply believes people would rather pay less for products than more. The company has used its considerable influence to continually drive down the cost of goods to the consumer. It is hard to argue with their logic and success.

The downside of this strategy is the increasing scrutiny that the company faces (and will face) in its role as the world's largest company. It has been under attack at various times for its labor practices (the company remains antiunion), the hiring of illegal immigrants, and discriminatory practices against women; its aggressive real estate growth has been criticized by communities, who think Wal-Mart is bad for other retailers, and by suppliers, who believe Wal-Mart simply exerts too much influence.

The threat for Wal-Mart probably lies as much in the court of public opinion as it does at the cash registers, where its formula seems unassailable. Could Wal-Mart be subject in the future to antitrust violations that have dogged giant corporations in the past? It seems unlikely, given that the company brings prices down, not up. But public sentiment could turn against them.

Our belief is that the consumer needs to be the ultimate judge in a free-market economy. As powerful as Wal-Mart is, Est shows that there are a number of companies who compete quite successfully with the behemoth today and that there will be plenty of ways to compete in the future. Dollar General builds stores in Wal-Mart's shadows; Target has taken a Hot-Est positioning; Whole Foods sells more fashionable food; and others have more compelling services or product propositions. To be sure, however, any conversation about the future of retailing must begin with the impact of Wal-Mart.

# A Glance at the Future

## Multichannel Retailing

We lived through the excessive hype of e-commerce and watched with great fascination the boom and the inevitable bust. Though no one really cares (or ever looks back at prognostications), we were seemingly the lone voice of reason against unrealistic growth numbers and projections for a future dominated by e-commerce.

Of course, we had a vested interest in bricks and mortar. In a sense, we could well have been accused as being the same dinosaurs as our retail clients. We had a different point of view, however—not based on bricks and mortar but based on a deep understanding and history of direct marketing. We understood the dynamics of catalog retailing and knew what worked and didn't work well in that medium.

We were rightly suspicious of a number of new concepts that failed to pay heed to the lessons learned by direct marketers long ago. This included which products are efficient to ship, which don't have high return rates, and so on. The absurdities raged on—from trying to efficiently ship 50-pound bags of dog food or 24 packs of toilet paper to e-commerce propositions based on businesses that were too small or not profitable or were otherwise at a disadvantage.

At the very same time, we were also huge believers of the power of electronic commerce. It has revolutionized retailing in a number of ways and will continue to do so. Not all of them, however, are directly related to commerce. In fact, we believe that e-commerce as we know it now will probably one day account for around 5 to 10 percent of all retail sales, which is an impressive number in itself. Combined with catalogs and other direct marketing vehicles, we see consumer direct growing to more than 15 percent of all retail sales. This is huge and significant—but does not spell the death of bricks-and-mortar stores as we know them.

We became very intrigued with the concept of "clicks and mortar" and were early in exploring the interrelationship between the mediums. This became known as multichannel retailing, and we believe that this is fast becoming one of the critical business drivers of the next decade.

Simply stated, multichannel retailers use all available mediums to reach the consumer in the way that the consumer wants to be approached. We know now (and suspected back then) that this means the consumer wants different approaches for different purposes. The groundbreaking work of our colleagues at the JC Williams Group definitively shows that the same customer *does* shop all channels and that there is a direct correlation between their behaviors: They may see an item in a catalog and purchase it online, see an item online and buy it at a retail store, or choose various other combinations. The multichannel shopper is the best customer that retailers will have.

Even if e-commerce comprises only 5 to 10 percent of total retail sales, its influence can be far greater.

- The Internet's power as a medium for information, as one example, is having profound changes on the relationships between retailer and consumer. The consumer can now come armed (to an auto dealer, let's say) with more information than the salesperson. Knowledge is indeed power.
- The ability of consumers to shop when they want and where they want signals a profound shift in power. The consumer no longer has to abide by retailers' rules and hours. They have global choice.
- We believe eBay to be the most revolutionary concept to hit retailing in the past several decades. It is the ultimate vehicle for putting the customer in control, developing one-to-one relationships between buyer and seller. Customers control what they are willing to pay, which is also a profound change, and eBay creates a continual flow of real-time information that drives market efficiencies. How can you build a retail

store more efficient than a Wal–Mart or a Costco? The truth is that you probably cannot. However, it is a different proposition from a cost standpoint if you have no store at all: The mom-and-pop merchants on eBay can sell for less because they have significantly less overhead to account for.

- Pushing the envelope on Easy-Est, e-tailers like Amazon have built brilliant, customer-friendly systems that learn what their customers are buying and adapt the product offers around those customers. Retail stores, by necessity, are built to be efficient for the masses: Amazon can tailor its mix to the individual.

Yes, the direct revenue impact of e-commerce will be considerable. But, we think the overall economic influence will be far greater. To date, retailers have done relatively little to take advantage of the power of multiple channels. We are amazed by how few take full advantage of all the mediums available: It is difficult to find evidence that many retailers even *have* a web site, let alone promote its benefits.

One of our longtime clients, Sears, is one of the better practitioners of multichannel selling. Again, while it drives considerable business online and continues to grow at a prodigious rate, one of the huge additional benefits is the ability to order on the Internet and pick up products in the store. Sears gains a huge benefit from this service well beyond the value of pure Internet sales. Additionally, the acquisition of Lands' End, one of the premier catalog/Internet retailers, strengthens its multichannel capabilities. While the core Sears business declined in 2003, its direct business grew at more than 40 percent.

Pottery Barn (part of Williams-Sonoma) is able to use its catalogs and Internet capabilities as a way to test new categories before making a commitment to retail stores. Right now, Pottery Barn is experimenting with PB Teen and West Elm. Both concepts might eventually become retail ideas, but the company can experiment at far less cost using the catalog medium. If it works, the company will know where its best customers are located and which products sell best, giving it a significant leg up on traditional retailers who find this out by trial and error. Equally important, the company looks at all available marketing tools, including its catalogs, to help drive business to all of its channels. The old ways of measuring catalog ROI are quickly becoming obsolete.

In the immediate future, we expect even more profound changes to happen to retail stores as companies fully integrate multichannel capabilities. This includes in-store pickup, real-time inventory information at the stores, and perhaps a dramatic restructuring of inventory needs at a retail level. Retailers need to develop the best approach to meeting consumer needs. Multichannel retailing will be a necessity for future success, not just something nice to have. The Internet and e-commerce are alive and well—just not exactly in the form some expected.

### Multiformats

Just as one channel retailing won't work very well in the future, neither will one-size-fits-all retailers. Retailers once excelled at building the same box, over and over again. Consistency was rewarded over flexibility—retailing metrics work very well when a retailer can build cookie-cutter formats.

What's changed? Plenty, it turns out. Part of this is a function of sheer size. Many established retailers have run out of traditional sites to open, having successfully conquered the major metropolitan markets and the suburban locations where real estate is plentiful. In order to grow further, these retailers need to examine markets they might once have ignored. This includes urban markets with high density but difficulties getting space to build a complete format. This could also include markets deemed too small to support their formats— small towns and rural locations with small overall sales potential.

# A Glance at the Future

Retailers are experimenting with multistory stores, express stores, and smaller footprints to tap into this potential.

The consumer has also profoundly changed. Among major changes in U.S. demographics, nearly one-third of the country is now non-Caucasian. Food retailers are experimenting with Hispanic formats that specifically cater to this audience. At a minimum, all retailers are adapting their formats to better address the particular needs of a trade area—from issues like the weather, ethnicity, and income to market-specific challenges: Are stores near the beach, a college campus, a freeway? Information technology is now replacing what gut feel used to provide—the ability to intelligently change merchandise to meet local market situations.

Finally, retailers are driven to grab a greater share of the overall market. Fashion retailers are slicing and dicing the market to finite degrees, getting more and more specific in reaching a particular target market. Subsegments are becoming increasingly precise. For example, Club Libby Lu (now owned by department store retailer Saks) targets the needs of girls ages three to seven; Janie and Jack (part of Gymboree) targets the birth to age three population. Teen retailers are also becoming more precise. It is not enough to target a general teen market. Retailers need to be more specific, addressing a surfing look or edgy teens.

Winning retailers will define the markets more precisely, developing formats and format extensions that better meet consumers' needs.

## Changing Roles of Suppliers and Retailers

One of the fascinating dynamics that will play out over the next 5 to 10 years is the changing role of retailers and suppliers. In the future, it will become very difficult to accurately determine what businesses they are really in.

The drivers of these changes are somewhat complex but eminently predictable. We can boil it down to a simple statement that takes into account the two overriding factors: "The company that controls the brand controls a greater percentage of the profits." This statement deals with the economic reality that the brand is typically entitled to a disproportionate share of margins and profits. Taking a more customer-centric view, controlling the brand also means that companies have a better ability to be closer to customers and respond more quickly to their needs.

Suppliers to the retail community are looking at the following dynamics:

- Market share among retailers has been consolidating. There are fewer companies to sell to, as we demonstrated in Chapter 9, Table 9.1. This means that risk is more highly concentrated among fewer accounts. Consider that the top three department store chains controlled nearly 82 percent of the business in 2002 and that the top three discounters controlled nearly 86 percent of the market. For many large suppliers, Wal-Mart alone might represent 25 percent or more of their total sales. These suppliers are looking for ways to mitigate risk.
- Retailers are asserting greater control of their brands. Private-label products are growing in the retail business, in all of its variations. This includes the traditional sense of private branding—offering less costly items and increasingly sophisticated brand programs that replicate the role of a national brand. Retailers like Target have brilliantly created captive or exclusive brands (Mossimo, Michael Graves, and Isaac Mizrahi). Large department store chains like Federated have developed their own brands successfully (e.g., INC) and are also leveraging their relationships with suppliers to launch exclusives (H by Tommy Hilfiger).
- Suppliers are being asked to take a greater degree of control over their products on the shelf. They are morphing into

category managers and category leaders and taking a more active interest in the total success of the category. Over time, this could blur the lines between supply and retail. Whereas suppliers used to own products until they hit the retailer's warehouse or back room, in the future they may own the product until the customer actually buys it.

From a retailer's perspective, branding has become the key buzzword, again, for somewhat obvious reasons:

- It is difficult to make a lot of money selling other people's brands. This is increasingly becoming true, as major forces like Wal-Mart continue to drive down costs and prices among nationally branded products. Private brands offer better margins and protected business.
- As retailers gain more control, they begin to exert the power of brands among their consumers. Where the traditional skills sets of retailers used to focus on being efficient distributors of other people's products, they are now evolving into brand marketers themselves. Target has done a brilliant job of assuming the role of brand developer and marketer. As a consequence, it is taking a greater share of the profits.
- Retailers will also move to increase the amount of direct sourcing. Not only are they becoming brand marketers, but many are assuming the role of product developers and procurers.

Retailers like Pottery Barn, RadioShack, The Gap, Sharper Image, Abercrombie & Fitch, and Crate & Barrel derive a significant portion of their sales from privately branded products. Are they retailers or brands? Coach drives over 60 percent of its sales through its own stores, and others, like Ralph Lauren and Bose, are more than 50 percent retail or consumer-direct focused. Are they suppliers or retailers? Mainstream retailers in every facet of retail, from drugstores and supermarkets to home improvement, are all actively increasing their penetration of exclusive products.

The skill sets needed to excel in retail versus a branded supplier business are radically different. The companies that can master both will be poised to take greater control of their brands and greater control of profits in the future.

### Technology

Retailers have access to an astounding array of technology to enable them to better analyze and plan their businesses.

- Most retailers can have real-time data on what's selling and what's not selling in their stores. The ever-increasing numbers of retailers with loyalty programs can tie product movement, sales history, and basket size to a particular customer. Wal-Mart has one of the largest storage facilities for transactional data in the world; only the federal government has more capacity.
- Sophisticated software is available to help retailers price their products and take appropriate markdowns. Category-management tools exist to optimize merchandise mix from a category level down through specific store sets for a given store.
- Analysis tools exist to help retailers determine exactly where to put stores and what their expected financial performance will be.
- Integrated database and customer relationship management (CRM) tools exist to help retailers coordinate their efforts across multiple channels and formats.
- Technology is here already, and breakthroughs in radio frequency identification (RFID) are on the way that will allow retailers to further streamline the supply chain. Already, many retailers and suppliers are exchanging information on sales

performance on a real-time basis to maximize sales productivity and throughput.

- Tools are in place, with more on the way, to assist customers through the buying process. Everything from self-help kiosks and checkouts to sophisticated wireless devices that can guide the customer through the aisle. Electronic shelf tags can communicate instant pricing updates.

Welcome to the era of scientific retailing. And welcome to tremendous confusion on behalf of the retailer. Retailers have access to stunning amounts of data, all of which can help them more effectively run their businesses. At the same time, few if any retailers are actually able to take advantage of the tools at their disposal. From a global standpoint, Tesco (the incredible British retailer) and Wal-Mart are probably leading the way. Most others are faced with the problem of too many priorities and not enough time and money to develop and integrate all the tools at their disposal. It has spawned a boom in consulting, as technology simply moves faster than the retailer's ability to effectively use it.

The winning retailers in the future will be masters of technology, able to effectively use these tools to streamline costs and better serve customers. Technology will never be an end-all solution, however. Retailing is still a combination of art and science—merchants who can use available tools to make better choices. Technology will never replace the role of merchants and their ability to make the right choices and connect with customers. Developing a balance between merchants' instincts and the vast array of technological advances will further separate winners and losers in the future.

### Consumer Will Still Rule

Of course, this is our bias, but we will state the case one more time. Winning retailers in the future will be paying close attention to the consumer, developing a compelling way to differentiate themselves from the competition in the consumer's mind. In short, they will have an Est proposition for the consumer that is both compelling and sustainable.

This won't be easy. The customer is more diverse than ever before, is more demanding, and has an infinite array of choices available. Consumers will leverage their power to reward retailers who get it right and to punish those who don't.

Winners will need to be more adept than ever at truly understanding what consumers are looking for and will need to respond to those needs at just the right time. Even if a retailer makes it to the top, the time it has to ride its concept will be shorter than ever. The customers will see to that.

In the end, it is all about serving the needs of customers and developing an Est proposition, whether it's winning on price (Cheap-Est); selection (Big-Est); fashion (Hot-Est); service (Easy-Est), or convenience (Quick-Est). Get it right and retailing can provide enormous sales and profits. Get it wrong and the Black Hole is waiting.

# NOTES

*Preface*

**page vii** "How did you go bankrupt?" "Gradually, then Suddenly."

Ernest Hemingway, *The Sun Also Rises* (NY: Charles Scribner's Sons, 1926).

*Chapter 3*

**page 46** For good measure, Merriam-Webster defines *Cheap* as "purchasable below the going price or the real value" or "charging or obtainable at a low price."

*Merriam-Webster's Dictionary* (Springfield, MA: Merriam-Webster, July 1994).

*Chapter 5*

**page 90** Gerald Storch, who was quoted in the April 2, 2001, issue of *DSN Retailing Today* saying, "Wal-Mart is the greatest retailer that ever was, and we have to compete with them on a regular basis. There is no one else that has been able to compete with Wal-Mart and thrive. Very few have been able to compete with them and survive."

# Notes

"Target Works Its Market Magic," *DSN Retailing Today,* vol. 40, no. 7, 2 April 2001, p. 64.

**page 95**  March 2000 cover story about a nationwide trend of the masses craving high-style design: "[Target] has become the talk of Madison Avenue, not to mention Main Street."

Frank Gibney, Jr., and Belinda Luscombe, "The Redesigning of America," *Time,* 20 March 2000.

**page 95**  In a similar vein, *Newsweek* devoted an ample portion of its October 2003 design issue to the advancements in fashion being made at Target.

Daniel McGinn, "Isaac Hits Target," *Newsweek,* 27 October 2003.

## Chapter 7

**page 127**  According to the 2001 survey of average service time done for *QSR Magazine* by Sparagowski & Associates, Wendy's was fastest at drive-through, with average service time of 2 minutes, 14.7 seconds. That's far better than number two Burger King, which managed an average time of 2 minutes, 42.2 seconds per customer. Chick-fil-A was next at 2 minutes, 47.2 seconds, followed by McDonald's at 2 minutes, 50.9 seconds. In the world of Quickest, seconds do indeed matter to the customer.

Laura Tutor, "Who Delivers in Drive-Thru," QSR Online, 2001, retrieved 20 January 2004 from www.qsrmagazine.com/drive-thru/2001/index.phtml.

**page 134**  A 1998 *New York Times* article about Walgreens began by then–Walgreen CEO L. Daniel Jorndt explaining how he paced off 440 yards from where he had recently parked his car at a Wal-Mart to the store's front entrance. "If you want a

# Notes

pack of razor blades or a stick of deodorant," Jorndt told the *Times* reporter, "The last place you want to go is a 150,000-square-foot mass merchant or the Mall of America."

David Barboza, "Private Sector: Keeping Walgreens on Main St., *New York Times,* 6 December 1998, late edition: sec. 3, p. 2, col. 4.

## Chapter 9

**page 164**  For every man, woman, and child in this country, there is now about 21 square feet of retail space, according to the National Research Bureau. That's nearly three times as much as there was in 1972, when there was only 7.9 square feet of retail space per capita.

Scope USA Total Leasable Retail Area of U.S. Shopping Centers (1970–2002). International Council of Shopping Centers web site, retrieved 20 January 2004 from www.icsc .org/srch/rsrch/scope/current/ScopeGraphs_total.gif.

## Chapter 11

**page 209**  Two professors, one from Columbia University and one from Stanford University, published a paper in the December 2000 issue of the *Journal of Personality and Social Psychology* that illustrated the perils of too much choice.

Sheena S. Iyengar and Mark R. Lepper, "When Choice Is Demotivating: Can One Desire Too Much of a Good Thing?" *Journal of Personality and Social Psychology,* vol. 79, no. 6, December 2000, pp. 995–1004.

**page 214**  According to Tom Heymann, Americans as a whole spend more than 100 million hours a day waiting in line.

Tom Heymann, *On an Average Day* (NY: Fawcett Columbine, 1989).

# INDEX

# Index

# Index

# Index

# Index

**249**

# Index

# Index

# Index

# Index

# Index

# Index

# Index